T0307967

Personal Midrash

Personal Midrash
Fresh Insights into the Torah

DANIEL H. SHULMAN

URIM PUBLICATIONS
Jerusalem • New York

Personal Midrash: Fresh Insights into the Torah
by Daniel H. Shulman
Copyright © 2017 Daniel Shulman

Printed in USA

First Edition

ISBN 978-965-524-267-6

Published by
Urim Publications
P.O. Box 52287,
Jerusalem 9152102
Israel
www.UrimPublications.com

Library of Congress Cataloging-in-Publication Data

Names: Shulman, Daniel H., author.
Title: Personal midrash : fresh insights into the Torah / Daniel H. Shulman.
Description: Jerusalem ; New York : Urim Publications, [2017] | Includes
   bibliographical references and index.
Identifiers: LCCN 2017026948 | ISBN 9789655242676 (hardcover : alk.
   paper)
Subjects: LCSH: Bible. Old Testament — Criticism, interpretation, etc.
Classification: LCC BS1178.H4 S577 2017 | DDC 222/.106 — dc23
LC record available at https://lccn.loc.gov/2017026948

CONTENTS

ACKNOWLEDGMENTS   9
INTRODUCTION   13

GENESIS (*Bereshit*) (בראשית)
  Bereshit   21
  Noah   22
  Lech Lecha   24
  Vayera   26
  Chaye Sarah   28
  Toledoth   30
  Vayetze   32
  Vayishlach   34
  Vayeshev   37
  Miketz   39
  Vayigash   41
  Vayechi   44

EXODUS (*Shemot*) (שמות)
  Shemot   49
  Va-ayra   51
  Bo   54
  Beshalach   56

Yitro   59
Mishpatim   62
Terumah   64
Tetzaveh   67
Ki-Tissa   69
Vayakhel   72
Pekudey   74

LEVITICUS (*Vayikra*) (ויקרא)
Vayikra   79
Tzav   81
Shemini   83
Tazria   85
Metzora   87
Acharei Mot   89
Kedoshim   91
Emor   93
Behar   95
Bechukotai   97

NUMBERS (*Bemidbar*) (במדבר)
Bemidbar   101
Naso   103
Behalotecha   105
Shelach Lecha   108
Korach   110
Chukat   113
Balak   115
Pinchas   117
Mattot   120
Massey   123

Deuteronomy (*Devarim*) (דברים)

Devarim	127
Va-Etchanan	129
Ekev	131
Re'eh	134
Shoftim	137
Ki-Tetze	139
Ki-Tavo	142
Nitzavim	146
Vayelech	147
Haazinu	149
Vezot Ha-Berachah	151

ACKNOWLEDGMENTS

I WRITE ONLY IN A PARTICULAR GENRE — AUTOBIOGRAPHY. This book is no different. It is impossible for me to reflect on this work without thinking about the inspirations and influencers, the audience and the adored, those who pushed me on and pulled me up. Nothing I write on these pages will do justice to their contributions. But, to paraphrase the Talmud (*Pirkei Avot*, 2:16), though I may not be required to give thanks adequately, I am not free to refrain from trying.

To Vic Feldman, whose generosity and support was foolish when I was a young, inexperienced patent lawyer, and whose generosity and support is equally misguided today. I am blessed you are such a poor judge of character and potential. Thank you for your support, generosity, faithfulness and loyalty. You literally made this book possible.

To Rabbis Carl Wolkin, Aaron Melman and Ari Averbach, and Cantor Steven Stoehr of Congregation Beth Shalom, my home synagogue of over thirty years, thank you for showing me trust and guidance. You have been sources of wisdom, friendship and learning throughout my adult life. Thank you also to David Barany, Director of Education at Congregation Beth Shalom, for your friendship and instincts. You taught me about the ecstasy of teaching.

To Kim Resnick, you loved me when I thought nobody could or would, and your love made me want to do great things with my life. I was born long before you came into my life, but I didn't begin living until we met. You forced me to look at myself and others from the inside out, to see people and ask, "What's on the inside?" You took my authentic Jewish curiosity and focused it on people, love and relationships. You didn't just start me on this Project. You started me on being me.

To Paula Avenaim, two years after laying down my pen, we met for lunch and I realized that to be the person I was telling you I was, I needed to finish this book. On the drive home in the rain, I saw the most perfect rainbow arched across the entire sky from one end of the horizon to the next. Our lunch was a sign. Thank you.

To Melisa Rosenthal, nobody used more wit, humor or admiration to move me than you did. You encouraged me by showing me that my life's demand for Jewish commitment deserved to be met with joyful effort. Thank you for showing me the proper spirit, and for expertly editing, proofing and checking this manuscript so I wouldn't embarrass myself.

To Dahlia Ronen, your five famous words, "Do what makes you happy," still ring in my ears. Your love, adoration, admiration and respect imbued me with the confidence to see this through. You have been my biggest fan, but also my most patient partner. It is not a stretch to say that I would not have even attempted to reach for my dreams without you. My love for you is everlasting. Thank you.

To Lisa Cohen, you convinced me that my words could touch hearts. Your love and friendship provided calm when the stirring of emotions paralyzed me, and provided passionate energy when ambivalence set in. Few could do either. Only you could do both. Thank you for seeing inside me and knowing instinctively what I needed from you, and when. You have been more than my best friend. You have been my most important friend.

Thank you to the team at Urim Publishing, who took my dream and put it into print.

And finally, but most importantly, none of this would have

happened but for the three greatest gifts in my life. Many men have the opportunity to be a father. None has enjoyed the awesomeness of the job as much as I have. To Elijah, Noah and Micah, you are my blessings and my reason for wanting to be who I am. I love you. This book is for you.

D.H.S.

INTRODUCTION

W HEN I GRADUATED FROM HIGH SCHOOL, I ASKED
for and received as a graduation gift from my parents
the ten-volume *Midrash Rabbah*.

You might think that this was an odd request for a public
school-educated Conservative Jew who had been suspended from
two different Hebrew schools and, when not suspended, spent most
of Hebrew school in the hallway or the rabbi's office. And, you'd
probably be right.

But, as it was, I headed off to college to study physics and math
(I eventually became a lawyer, so you can see for yourself how
that turned out). While there, I studied the *Midrash Rabbah*, every
volume, cover to cover. Two things happened. First, I became enam-
ored with the process, boldness and authenticity (more on that in
a bit) of midrash. I became fascinated by the sages of old who were
able to weave stories and explanations together, seamlessly going
from one point in Scripture to another, in a time when a searchable
electronic database of the Bible did not exist. Their knowledge
of scripture was astounding, and frankly, seemed inhuman (and
unfair). Second, I deepened an already consuming curiosity about
Judaism, and Scripture in particular. Northwestern University,
having its historical background as a seminary, as well as being a
world class university with abundant library resources, provided all
the resources I could ever imagine to feed what was then (if not still

now) an insatiable thirst for knowledge. I devoured every footnote and every reference, tracking from library stack to library stack, and even from library to library, to locate works – from the common, like Maimonides *Mishneh Torah*, to the esoteric, like *Sefer Yetzirah*. I had time (as a physics and math student, I made an excellent lawyer), and I devoted it to learning everything I could about Judaism.

That was twenty years ago.

While my interest never waned, my time and dedication to learning did. Adulthood, work, parenthood and, well, life got in the way. Some fifteen years after graduating college, I was spending time with a friend going through her own process of Jewish discovery. I assumed the role of discussion partner, if not teacher, but in my heart, I still wanted to be a student. At the very least, I wanted to believe that I had something original to teach. With her encouragement, I began writing midrash. I would call it simply, my "Project."

This book, an original midrash for each of the 54 Torah portions, is the culmination of that Project.

*

You may ask yourself what qualifies me to write midrash (putting aside the fundamental question of "what" exactly midrash is, and whether that's even an accurate description of what I was doing). The answer to what qualifies me is nothing more than an "*authentic Jewish curiosity.*" In fact, returning to the question of "what" midrash is, my best answer is that midrash is a personal, but quintessentially Jewish response to our curiosity about the Torah. Midrash is the cure for an *authentic Jewish curiosity*. (I promised I would get to it).

What is so authentically Jewish about our curiosity about the Torah? My answer, in short, is everything. Let's think about what we do when we engage in midrash, when we interpret, explain and boldly – because a certain boldness is required – add to the Torah.

So let's start with this: why create midrash? It is because the Torah is both fundamentally authoritative, and also in need of interpretation. It is both revealed and hidden. It is (so we choose to believe) written by God, and yet incomplete. Think of how *bold* we must be to engage in common midrashic activities. We rearrange letters. We add completely unwritten stories to the narrative. We recast passages to find unobvious (sometimes opposite) meanings. We treat the rest of Scripture as a tool to reinterpret the Torah, as if it were a seamless whole. We pull things out of context (unashamedly) to give new meaning. And, we do this to a text that is *canonical*. It is authoritative. Not to be changed. Official. To be obeyed. And yet, we treat it like it is full of errors and unintended consequences. This *reverence* (for we only do this because we so revere the Torah) combined with this *irreverent approach* is a function of *authentic Jewish curiosity*. No other faith would allow such an approach to Scripture. For Jews, it is fundamental.

So what qualifies me to write midrash? Nothing and everything. I have no formal training. I'm not a rabbi or a scholar. I have a little knowledge of Hebrew, and plenty of books and references (my library has expanded considerably since the *Midrash Rabbah*). Yet none of that gives me any special qualification. Instead, I claim only to have an *authentically Jewish curiosity*.

*

Before I share my midrashim with you, allow me to tell you about my process. My Project was to write one, and only one midrash per portion (I'm not a masochist, after all). I was not trying to explain the whole portion, or find an overriding theme, or create an entire *dvar Torah*. I read the portion thoroughly, and I made notes of passages that are unclear, troubling, curious (there's that word again), out of place, or awkward. Sometimes I found just a few, sometimes many. Eventually, I began to narrow down to the one I would focus on, or if I could relate them, maybe two. At that point, I tried to find some hidden meaning to explain my curiosity. The passage may have been important to the overall theme of the portion, or it may have been completely peripheral. But hopefully, the interpretation was original.

Essential to this process (as you will see as you read them) was to read the Torah in its original Hebrew, with a useful translation. My knowledge of Hebrew is basic. It's better than most, but in no way would I characterize myself a fluent speaker. I would struggle to carry on a Hebrew conversation. Most of the Hebrew I needed to know for my Project I learned through a lifetime of following along during prayer services and reading the Torah in translation. Certain words, word forms and idioms appear over and over in Biblical and liturgical Hebrew (much of which is Biblical). Recognizing those helped.

I also noted the need for a "useful" translation. The Hebrew Bible is a linguistic enigma. Aside from the fact that many words are unknown outside the Biblical context, the usage of many words is awkward. The Torah is ancient. Its grammar is ancient. Its spellings are ancient. Even for modern Hebrew readers, reading the Torah is like a modern English reader reading Chaucer's *Canterbury Tales*. It can be done, but it takes effort. Many modern translations gloss over that difficulty of language to present a more "readable" translation. Those translations would have made my process more difficult, rather than easier. What I needed was a translation whose English translation was awkward when the Hebrew was awkward. At least then I could read it, catch something amiss, and go back to the Hebrew to unpack it. So often, that unpacking of an awkward Hebrew phrase opened up the world of midrash. In my case, I found the Hertz Chumash to be the perfect resource.[1]

Other tools were also invaluable. I had the five-volume Reuven

---

1. *The Pentateuch and Haftorahs*, Rabbi J.H. Hertz, ed; Soncino Press (2nd ed., 1960). This is not a criticism of Rabbi Hertz. I have to believe that his sometimes awkward translations were intentional. If not, well, as the saying goes, "*Az der talmid iz a voiler, iz der rebbi oich a voiler*" ("If the student is successful, the teacher gets the praise").

Alcalay Hebrew-English Dictionary,[2] at least until I became com-
fortable with Google Translate. To search the entire Hebrew Bible,
I had the searchable Soncino Talmud with Tanach installed on my
computer. Again, that sufficed until technology caught up by pro-
viding various searchable Tanach apps on my smartphone. Late in
the process, I even found a *gematria*[3] app that, to my amazement
(and increased efficiency) would find words – and even entire
Biblical phrases – whose numerical equivalent would add up to a
particular number. You will see that gematria was a common midrashic tool of mine.

   With tools in hand, my typical process was as follows: read the
portion, making notes along the way of each curiosity. The first
step would be to find the curiosity I thought *most* curious, or at
least having the most potential to be interesting (this was, of course,
wholly subjective, in addition to involving a substantial amount of
guesswork since I could not really be sure where the midrash would
go). At that point, depending on the curiosity, I might go in any
number of directions. I would try to identify a particular Hebrew
word, phrase or concept that seemed important or critical to the
curiosity. I evaluated it. I searched Scripture for its uses. I rearranged
the letters. I substituted other words for words having a numerical
equivalent. I examined the context for clues. Most of the time, I
took a break and came back to it later. I tried to find something that
seemed to fit a theme that answered the question the curiosity had

---

2. Alcalay, Reuben, *The Complete English-Hebrew, Hebrew-English Dictionary (5 Vols.)*,
P. Shalom Pubs. (1996).
3. *Gematria* is the process by which a numerical value is assigned to each Hebrew letter. The first nine letters of the Hebrew alphabet, א (aleph) through ט (tet), are given
the values 1 through 9, respectively. The next nine letters, י (yud) through צ (tsade),
are given the values 10 through 90, by tens (i.e., 10, 20, 30, etc.). The final four letters,
ק (kof) through ת (tav), are assigned 100 to 400, by hundreds (i.e., 100, 200, 300, etc.).
In that way, each word or phrase of Hebrew letters is assigned a value through gematria by summing the values of the letters.

raised. If I did find something I thought was unique, I would check my sources: *Midrash Rabbah*, Rashi's commentary, and others. If I found that someone, somewhere, had already thought of what I had written, I would start over. Above all, I wanted to be original.

And sometimes, I would get stumped and pick a different curiosity, starting the process all over.

In the end, I'm not sure what is more interesting – the midrash or the process by which I came to it. Ultimately, I included both here. You can choose just to read the midrashim, or read them with the commentary (a kind of "commentary on the commentary"). For some, the midrash may be sufficiently clear and interesting so that reading about how it came to be, might lessen its impact. No need to see how the sausage (or all-beef Kosher hot dog) is made.

So, allow me to share some midrashim with you.

בראשית

(Bereshit)

GENESIS

BERESHIT

WHY DOES THE TORAH START WITH THE LETTER ב (bet)? One would think that it should start with א (aleph)?

It is to teach us that when it comes to Creation, the matter is closed on all sides except going forward, but as to that, the matter is completely open to us. This is identical to the structure of the letter ב (bet), which is closed on the top, bottom and back, but open in the front (keeping in mind that Hebrew is read from right to left). But could not the Torah start with כ (kaf) and teach the same lesson?

If it had started with כ (kaf), one might believe that some plurality of things preceded Creation. Therefore, it starts with ב (bet) to teach us that prior to Creation, there was only One.

Notes

I have to confess, the idea of the Torah starting with ב (bet) is well-known, especially in Kabbalistic literature. So, I guess I started slowly. What occurred to me, however, was that the explanation for starting with ב (bet) applied equally well to כ (kaf), and so I dug a little deeper for a further explanation.

NOAH

IT IS WRITTEN: "AND NOAH WENT IN, AND HIS SONS, AND his wife, and his sons' wives with him, into the ark, *because of the waters of the flood* (מי המבול)" (Gen. 7:7).

Why does it say "because of the waters of the flood," when surely he went in because God had commanded him? How do we know that, in reality, Noah went into the ark at God's commandment? The Torah refers to "the waters (מי)" where one would otherwise expect it to say "waters (מים)." Thus, these particular "waters (מי)" must have been unique. And indeed they were. The waters of the flood (מי המבול) were specifically created by God to destroy those that deny Him, as it is written, "For the horses of Pharaoh went in with his chariots and with his horsemen into the sea, and the LORD brought back the waters (מי) of the sea upon them" (Ex. 15:19).

Notes

The thing that troubled me about this parasha was the idea, expressed above, that Noah would go into the ark because the water had gotten so high, as opposed to going in because God had told him to. It seemed like Noah didn't trust God that the flood would come, so only when it became clear that the water was too high to survive that he went into the ark. That seemed to demonstrate a stunning lack of faith. In studying the passage, the odd Hebrew spelling of "waters" gave a clue. Searching, I found the same usage in relation to the passage about Pharaoh. That provided the link to put the two passages together.

LECH LECHA

SCRIPTURE WARNS US AGAINST OVERZEALOUS PUBLIC worship of God. How do we know this? Because of what happened to Nadab and Abihu (Lev. 10). How else do we know that overzealous public worship of God causes a separation between us and Him? Because of what happened to our father, Abraham.

It is written (Gen. 12:7): "And the LORD appeared unto Abram." And what did Abraham do? He built an altar there, as it is written, "and he built there an altar unto the LORD, who appeared unto him."

Next the Torah tells us that Abraham journeyed from there to a spot between Beth-El and Ai, "and he built there an altar unto the LORD, and called upon the name of the LORD" (Gen. 12:8). We find that Abraham was overzealous in building an altar and calling upon God from this second site, even though God had not called to him from there first. What was the result of Abraham's overzealousness? Abraham was uprooted (נסע) from his connection to God, as it is written, "And Abram journeyed, going still toward (ונסוע) the South" (Gen. 12:9). What was the punishment that followed? "And there was a famine in the land" (Gen. 12:10).

But is it not written to continuously seek the LORD? How could Abraham be punished? It is because God desires that we are overzealous in our seeking him "with all thy heart and with all thy soul" (Deut. 4:29), that is, internally, but not externally. Therefore we must be attentive to God's call, even when seeking Him, so as to be one with God upon His call, as it is written, "Listen to me, you who follow after righteousness, you who seek the LORD; look to the rock from where you have been cut, and to the hole of the pit from where you have been dug. Look to Abraham your father, and to Sarah who gave birth to you; for he was only one when I called him, and blessed him, and increased him" (Isa. 51:1–2). Abraham was "only one" when God called him, but not when He did not.

How do we know that even Abraham accepted that his second altar had been disfavored? Because when he returned from Egypt, he did not worship at the second altar between Beth-El and Ai, but instead waited until he came to the first altar, which had been where God appeared to him, as it says, "And he went on his journeys from the South even to Beth-El, unto the place where his tent had been at the beginning, between Beth-El and Ai; unto the place of the altar, *which he had made there at the first*; and Abram called *there* on the name of the LORD" (Gen. 13:3–4).

Notes

Abram's frequent altar building seemed odd. Given the historical context, it really isn't all that strange that a religious person in those days would build altars, but the Torah hadn't really introduced the concept yet among any of the pre-Abraham generations. So, something seemed significant about it. Two additional things piqued my interest. First, a famine ensued just after his altar-building, and famine almost always has a negative connotation in Scripture (as in a punishment of some sort). Second, when Abram returned along the same route, he didn't stop where he had made the second altar. In fact, the Torah pointedly states that he returned to the first altar. That distinction led to exploring the difference between the two altar building exercises. The reference to Abraham in Isaiah fit the story perfectly.

VAYERA

W HY DOES ABRAHAM ARGUE WITH GOD TO SPARE the lives of the evil, but does not argue at all over the life of the innocent (Isaac)?

"How precious also are your thoughts to me, O God! How vast is their sum" (Ps. 139:17)! From this we learn that Abraham would interpret God's visions to him through numbers, for it follows, "If I should count them, they are more in number than the sand; when I awake, I am still with you" (Ps. 139:18). Similarly, it was said to Abraham, "Look now toward heaven, and count the stars, if you are able to count them" (Gen. 15:5).

Scripture relates, "And He said, 'Take *now* (נא) your son, your only son Isaac, whom you love'" (Gen. 22:2). What was meant by "נא"? Abraham understood (נא 51) to mean המאה ("the 100") (5+40+1+5=51). This refers to Isaac's forthcoming blessing, for with respect to Isaac it is written: "And Isaac sowed in that land, and found in the same year a *hundredfold*; and the LORD blessed him" (Gen. 26:12). Therefore, while Isaac's fate was sealed, with Sodom and Gomorrah their fates was not yet sealed, as it is written, "I *will* go down now, and see whether they have done altogether according to the cry which has come to me; and if not, I *will* know" (Gen. 18:21).

Thus did Abraham not argue, believing that Isaac would in any event survive to that year when he would be blessed, as it is written,

"I will multiply your seed as the stars of the heaven, and as the sand which is upon the sea shore . . . and in thy seed shall all the nations of the earth be blessed" (Gen 22:17–18). Because Abraham heard the reference to Isaac's *hundredfold* blessing in his call, he no longer doubted Isaac's survival. Therefore did Abraham answer, "How precious also are your thoughts to me, O God! How vast is their sum! If I should count them, they are more in number than the sand; when I awake, I am still with you" (Ps. 139:18).

Notes

This was one of the first midrash I ever wrote. Telling the story of the Akedah on Rosh Hashanah, our Rabbi would always point out that Abraham didn't argue to protect Isaac. This contrasted with his argument over Sodom and Gomorrah. There, he was willing to save the evil to protect the innocent (if they existed), but with his own son, he didn't question God at all. To be sure, the Akedah is a fundamentally difficult story that, in many ways, defies explanation. And, even now, I'm not sure my midrash helps shed any spiritual light on the story; if Abraham never feared for Isaac's life, that changes the entire lesson of the story. Still, Abraham's silent acquiescence to God's horrific command demands an explanation, even today.

CHAYE SARAH

IT IS WRITTEN, "AND SARAH DIED IN KIRIATH-ARBA (בקרית
ארבע) – the same is Hebron" (Gen. 23:2). Why was she in Hebron
while Abraham was dwelling in Beer-Sheba (Gen. 22:19), as it
is written, "And Abraham *came* to mourn for Sarah" (Gen. 23:2)?

She had heard Abraham was going to sacrifice her only son, Isaac,
and raced to Hebron – the location of the altar she was aware of
where the angels of God had told her about the coming of Isaac
(Gen. 13:18). When she didn't find them there (because they had
gone to Mount Moriah), she was overcome with grief and died.

How do we know that Sarah's grief clouded her judgment, so that
she died without understanding what had happened to Isaac? Read
"And Sarah died in Kiriath-Arba (בקרית ארבע)" as "And Sarah died in
a morning of an excessive cloud (בקר יתר עב) as it is written, "Do you
know the marvels worked upon the expanse of clouds (עב), by Him
whose understanding is perfect?" (Job 37:16).

Notes

*There were quite a few things in this parasha I had thoughts about.
In verse 12, there is a phrase about Eliezer (Abraham's servant sent to
find Isaac a wife) that he "ha[d] all goodly things of his master's in his*

hand." The idea that I could unpack that statement to discover what were Abraham's "goodly things" was tantalizing – why Abraham was picked among all men to be the beginning of God's covenant is one of the great untold mysteries of the Torah (though one of the great sources of midrash as well). At a later point, in verse 40, Eliezer paraphrases a statement he attributes to Abraham referring to "the LORD before whom I walk." Only Abraham never said any such thing. Matters like that scream out for an explanation. Ultimately, though, the fact that Sarah and Abraham were separated at her death was too full of meaning to ignore. On top of that, the Torah's mentioning of alternative names for a location, "Hebron" and "Kiriath-Arba" meant something more was to be discovered. Focusing on "Kiriath-Arba," I played with the letters to try to find a different meaning, eventually arriving at the above midrash.

TOLEDOTH

THE TORAH TELLS US THAT ISAAC RE-DUG EACH OF THE wells that his father had previously dug (Gen. 26:18). However, each time Isaac's servants dug a well, there was strife with the herdsmen of Gerar (Gen. 26:19–21). When Isaac dug the wells on his own, there was no strife (Gen. 26:22). How do we know that the servants sowed the strife with Isaac?

In each case in which a well is dug, the Torah uses the word "יחפר." However, when Isaac's servants dig the well in Beersheba, the Torah uses the word "יכרו." Now, Abraham had already been at Beersheba, and surely would have dug a well there, so why did Isaac's servants dig the well at Beersheba instead of Isaac himself? It was an additional well that they intended to be a pit in which to trap Isaac, as every instance of the word "כרו" in Scripture tells of harm to befall the righteous:

- "The insolent have dug (כרו) pits for me, flouting your teaching" (Ps. 119:85).
- "They dug (כרו) a pit for me, but they fell into it" (Ps. 57:7).
- "Yet they have dug (כרו) a pit for me" (Jer. 18:20).
- "For they have dug (כרו) a pit to trap me" (Jer. 18:22).

Thus were his servants surprised when their pit turned out to be a well, that they reported, "We have found water" (Gen. 26:32). Here the Torah speaks of the well – that same well – which they had dug, only now it uses the word "חפרו," because Isaac was safe from it.

Notes

Before getting to the digging of the wells, I considered a few other oddities. In relation to Isaac's prayers for Rebekah, the Torah says, "And the LORD let Himself be entreated of him" (Gen. 25:21). I thought that characterization of God's receptiveness to prayer interesting. Also fascinating was the reference to Abraham as having "kept My charge, My commandments, My statutes and My laws" (Gen. 26:5). Aside from circumcision, what could those be? But ultimately, the frequent digging and re-digging of the wells had to mean something. There was plenty to "dig into." The different parties involved in the digging and the different words used indicated something to interpret. Searching on the word "כרו" and finding the references in Jeremiah, and then Psalms, gave the context.

VAYETZE

"AND MOSES WAS 120 YEARS OLD WHEN HE DIED; HIS EYE was not dim, nor his natural force (לחה) abated" (Deut. 34:7). How do we know that this was so remarkable of Moses, that for other prophets, prophecy abated their natural force (לח)?

We learn this from the sequence of Jacob's famous dream. Of Jacob it is told:

"Jacob lay down (וישכב) in that place to sleep" (Gen. 28:11). Next, Jacob has his dream, during which the LORD stands beside him and speaks to him (Gen. 28:13–15). Next, Jacob awakes out of his sleep and declares, "Surely the LORD is in this place; and I knew it not" (Gen. 28:16). Even more so, he continues, "How full of awe is this place! This is none other than the house of God, and this is the gate of heaven" (Gen. 28:17). After all this, the Torah then tells us, "And Jacob rose up (וישכם) early in the morning" (Gen. 28:18).

Why does the Torah tell us that Jacob "rose up" after he had already awakened? Did he declare those things while lying on his back? Surely he was already awake. It is to teach us that God needed to restore his natural force לח (=38) which had been abated between the time he lay down (וישכב) and when he rose up (וישכם) (the difference between וישכם and וישכב = 38).

32

Notes

Jacob's first interactions with God are fascinating. First, God references "Abraham thy father," rather than Isaac. Jacob also seems genuinely overwhelmed with amazement, so much so that he seems to hallucinate, leading to statements like, "none other than the house of God and gate of Heaven." All of this seemed related to the odd sequence of his dreams . . . he seemed to always be between lying down and standing, and making proclamations all the while. He was talking while lying down, while rising up, while asleep and while awake. In fact, the encounter goes like this:

1. Jacob lays down
2. Jacob dreams
3. The LORD stands beside him and makes promises
4. Jacob wakes up
   a. He says, "Surely the LORD was in this place and I knew it not."
   b. He is afraid
5. Jacob rises up
6. Jacob makes promises to God

Jacob's encounter with God was . . . mystical. Trying to decipher the passage, I focused on the words for "lay down (וישכב)" and "rose up (וישכם)," and found the difference was 38. The easiest Hebrew word I could make with "38" was "לח," so I searched that and found the passage about Moses. The idea of the abating of natural force seemed thematically to fit.

VAYISHLACH

"AND JACOB ASKED HIM, AND SAID, 'TELL ME, I PRAY thee, thy name.' And he said, 'Wherefore is it that thou dost ask after my name?' And he blessed him there" (Gen. 32:30). Why does the Torah not tell us the blessing?

This was to teach us that Jacob was not fit to receive the blessing. How do we know that he was not fit? Because he was overly concerned about his own life in anticipation of the meeting with Esau. Thus does the Torah tell us, "And he took them, and sent them over the stream, and sent over that which he had. And Jacob was left alone" (Gen. 32:24–25). Therefore, after Jacob wrestles with the angel, he proclaims, "*My life* (נפש) is preserved" (Gen. 32:31).

Therefore does Scripture tell us, "He renews my life (נפש); He guides me in right paths as befits His name" (Ps. 23:3). Because the angel would not tell him his name, we know Jacob was not befitting His name, and therefore not fit for the blessing.

When did Jacob become fit for his blessing? When he was with his whole family, as it is written, "So Jacob came to Luz, which is in the land of Canaan – the same is Beth-El – *he and all the people that were with him*" (Gen. 35:6). Only then does God appear and tell Jacob his name (God Almighty), and we are told his blessing.

The importance of the name of God to Jacob's blessing is further reinforced in Jacob's response to the blessing from God, as the Torah tells us, "And Jacob called the name of the place where God spoke

with him there (ויקרא יעקב את שם המקום אשר דבר אתו שם אלהים), Beth-El"
(Gen. 35:15). But the "there (שם)" is superfluous. Therefore read,
"And Jacob called the name of the place where a name of God (שם
אלהים) spoke with him, Beth-El."

Notes

*Again, Jacob's encounters with God are exceedingly mysterious. In this
parasha, I noted many passages that spoke about Jacob being left alone,
or his intentional separation from his family. Initially, Jacob takes his
wives and sons and passes over the "ford of Jabbok" (Gen. 32:23), only to
be repeated in the next verse that he sent his family and all he has across
the stream. (Gen. 32:24). What was he sending seeing as he had already
crossed? We are then immediately told that Jacob was left alone. (Gen.
32:25). This called to mind for me the Creation story, where God observes,
"It is not good for man to be alone." Other odd passages: God tells Jacob
to "be fruitful and multiply" (Gen 35:11). Hadn't he had enough children
already?! God tells Jacob to go to Beth-El and "make there an altar to God"
(Gen. 35:1). Why does God refer to himself in the third person, and then
not be one of His specific names (such as LORD, or El Shaddai)? Why does
Jacob name the place "El-Beth-El?" Finally, God tells him his new name
is Israel, then "He called his name Israel." But the angel he had wrestled
with had already renamed him. Why then rename him again?*

*What struck me most, however, was the aftermath of the most famous
of Jacob's encounters with God – the wrestling. After, we are told merely,
"He [the angel with whom Jacob wrestled] blessed him there." I seriously
wanted to know: What was the blessing? In addition to the absence of
the actual blessing, the aftermath of the wrestling encounter is known
for Jacob inquiring as the man's/angel's name. Jacob is, of course, not
told. So, two things were unknown: the content of the blessing, and the
counterpart's name.*

Turning to the Hebrew, there was an abundance of clues. First, the statement that Jacob was attempting to preserve his life pervaded the parasha. He was fleeing Esau, and was alone to protect his family from Esau. Aside from physical loneliness, the phrase "נפשי" ("my spirit") indicated a personal possessive of his spirit, a spiritual loneliness. Second, the prevalence of the issue of "names," from the angel's lack of one to Jacob's new one, suggested looking into the Hebrew word for "name," or "שם." The word in Hebrew, depending on the vowels, is either "sheim," meaning "name," or "sham," meaning "there." Which word would depend on whether the vowel is a "tsere" (a long "a" sound) or a "kamatz" (more of an "aw" sound). But the Torah is written without vowels, letting the interpretation freely go in either direction. That connection was enough to complete the midrash.

VAYESHEV

"THERE IS THE CRUELTY OF FURY, THE OVERFLOWING of anger, but who can withstand envy (קנאה)" (Prov. 27:4)? The overpowering capacity for evil acts brought about by envy is exemplified in the story of Joseph.

Three times the Torah tells us that Joseph's brothers hated him:

- "And when his brethren saw that their father loved him more than all his brethren, they hated him, and could not speak peaceably unto him" (Gen. 37:4).
- "And Joseph dreamed a dream, and he told it to his brethren; and they hated him yet the more" (Gen. 37:5).
- "And they hated him yet the more for his dreams, and for his words" (Gen. 37:8).

Thus, as long as they hated him, they were motivated only to evil words ("[they] could not speak peaceably unto him.")

However, after Joseph tells his dream to his father and his brothers, their hate turns to envy. The common translation of the passage the Torah states, is, "And his brethren envied him, but his father kept the saying in mind (שמר את הדבר)." What does this statement really mean?

It is written: "ויקנאו בו אחיו ואביו שמר את הדבר". We should read the word "שמר" as an imperative, not past tense, so that the proper translation is, "And his brethren envied him and his father – safeguard (שמר) the word (את הדבר)!" What word should one safeguard, so as not to let it influence you, but "envy (יקנאו)!" For so great was Joseph's brothers' envy, for both Joseph and their father, that they were inspired to evil deeds, namely to want to kill Joseph.

Notes

Just about every passage in this parasha involved Joseph and words. The more he spoke, the more trouble he got into. This was hinted at early in the parasha when we are told that his brothers "could not speak peaceably unto him." The progression in the parasha is as follows: (1) Joseph brings an evil report (Gen. 37:2), (2) they hated him (Gen. 37:4), (3) they hated him more (Gen. 37:5), (4) they hated his words (Gen. 37:8), and finally (5) they envy him (Gen. 37:11). The interesting thing about the progression to envy, was Jacob was aware of it. The same verse says, "but his father kept the saying in mind" (Gen. 37:11). This is an occasion where the Hertz translation helped.[1] Others translated it "but his father kept the matter in mind," which might not have been so curious. The reference to "the saying" hinted at an awkwardness in the language that might provide a deeper understanding. And, I needed a proof-text for the idea I had taken from that progression, namely, that envy inspired more danger than mere hate. There were many passages in Scripture that fit (Prov. 6:34 was another one I didn't use).[2] Once I found that, the rest came together.

---

1. See Introduction, page iii.
2. "For envy is the rage of a man; and he will not spare in the day of vengeance" (Prov. 6:34).

MIKETZ

W HAT DOES JOSEPH INTEND WHEN HE TELLS JUDAH, "But as for you, get you up *in peace* unto your father" (Gen. 44:17)? He intended that the reunification of the brethren would restore to Jacob his trust in prophecy, which Jacob had lost, for Jacob's visions were accompanied by a lack of peace.

How do we know that after Joseph was sold away, Jacob's visions were accompanied by a lack of peace? The Torah tells us, "Now Jacob saw (217 = וירא) that there was corn in Egypt" (Gen. 42:1). But when Jacob communicated this to his sons, he added to it quarrel (תגר), misfortune (תברא) and confusion (שגש) (each equal to 603), as the Torah tells us, "And he said, 'Behold, I have heard (= שמעתי 820) that there is corn in Egypt'" (Gen. 42:2). Why does he tell his sons that he "heard" there is corn when we have been told that he "saw" it? Because the difference between those words is 603, which means Jacob's vision came with quarrel (תגר), misfortune (תברא) and confusion (שגש). What is the opposite of quarrel, misfortune and confusion? Surely it is peace. Therefore, when Joseph realized what had befallen Jacob, he endeavored to bring peace unto him, so that his visions could be understood without quarrel, misfortune and confusion; and immediately Joseph revealed himself to his brothers (Gen. 45:1).

How was it therefore proven that the bringing back of the brothers, the sons of Israel, brought back Jacob's trust in prophecy?

Because it says, "the spirit (רוח) of Jacob their father revived" (Gen. 45:27). This is what Scripture means when it says, upon the reunification of the exiled of Israel's offspring, "And I will not hide my face any more from them; for I have poured out my spirit (רוח) upon the house of Israel, says the LORD God" (Ezek. 39:29).

Notes

There were some additional things in this parasha I initially thought about. Why did God communicate with Pharaoh? Why did Joseph take an Egyptian wife? When Joseph is said to "fear God," shouldn't that have been a clue to his brothers, i.e., what would a believer of the God of their fathers (who, as far as we know, was likely unknown outside of Abraham's tribe and certainly not in the Egyptian court) be doing in Egypt, ranked just below Pharaoh?

What I came back to, though, was an inconsistency in the language. When that happens, the "midrashic" way of thinking is that the Torah is saying something important. So, when the Torah says Jacob "saw" corn in Egypt, why does he say instead to his sons that he "heard" there was corn in Egypt? Those statements needed to be reconciled by reading between the lines, i.e., a perfect source for midrash.

I have to admit, this midrash was a laborious exercise. I used gematria to calculate the difference between the two words, and having done that, I put as many three letter combinations together as I could to make 603.[1] Not being entirely well-versed in Hebrew, the letter combinations were really random; I spent hours looking in the dictionary to see if any of them actually made a word. Fortunately, I found three, and they each seemed to work with the theme I was developing.

---

1. Most words in the Hebrew language arise from a two or three letter root, with additional letters or spelling alterations having to do with verb conjugation, plurals, gender sense, and other grammatical rules.

VAYIGASH

W HY DOES JACOB NOT ALLOW HIMSELF TO ENJOY his reuniting with Joseph? Time and again, Jacob seems to wallow in self-pity, even when faced with the miraculous news that his long lost son is still alive. Thus, Jacob twice references his own death in the context of seeing Joseph (Gen. 45:28; Gen. 46:30). He shows no joy to Pharaoh when asked about his life, instead complaining, "Few and hard have been the years of my life, nor do they come up to the life spans of my fathers during their sojourns" (Gen. 47:9).

However, all of this can be explained when we realize that the news of Joseph's well-being was accompanied by news of a future tragedy. What was that tragedy? It was the future exile of the Jews from Israel, from which much of Israel would be permanently lost. From what do we infer this?

First, in God's call to Jacob immediately upon setting out to reunite with Joseph, God tells Jacob, "I will make you there into a great nation. I will go down with you to Egypt, and I will also bring you back" (Gen. 46:3–4). Why does God say to Jacob, "I will also bring *you* back" when he should have said, referring to the "great nation," "I will also bring *them* back?" It is because only a portion of Jacob's children was destined for redemption. How did Jacob know this? Because Joseph had foretold it to his brothers, and his brothers relayed it to Jacob. Joseph had said, "And God sent me before you to give a *remnant* (שארית) on the earth, and to save you alive for a great deliverance" (Gen. 45:7). To what did Joseph refer? To the period after the exile, as it is written (Isa. 10:20-22),

> "And in that day,
> The *remnant* (שאר) of Israel
> And the escaped of the House of Jacob
> Shall lean no more upon him that beats it,
> But shall lean sincerely
> On the LORD, the Holy One of Israel.
> Only a *remnant* (שאר) shall return,
> Only a *remnant* (שאר) of Jacob,
> To Mighty God.
> Even if your people, O Israel,
> Should be as the sands of the sea,
> Only a *remnant* (שאר) of it shall return."

Notes

Unlike the previous midrash, this one was straightforward. In the Introduction, I mentioned going to college at Northwestern University. In addition to the math and science courses I struggled through, I did utilize my electives to pursue some Jewish and Biblical studies more formally. One of the classes I took was on the Book of Isaiah. One of the dominant themes of Isaiah is the idea of the "remnant" of Israel that will return from the Exile.[1] Having recognized the reference to the "remnant" in Joseph's statement, I went straight to Isaiah 11 and made the connection.

---

1. Likely the Babylonian Exile, but perhaps the exile of the Northern Kingdom. It depends which "Isaiah" we're talking about – the Isaiah who primarily authored Chapters 1–39 (alive during the time of the exile of the Northern Kingdom by the

Assyrians in 722 B.C.E.), or so-called Deutero-Isaiah (alive during the end of the exile of Judah following the destruction of the First Temple by the Babylonians in 586 B.C.E.), who authored Chapters 40–66 (or Chapters 40–55, depending on if you are of the scholarly camp that believes there was a Trito-Isaiah who authored Chapters 56–66). The at least dual authorship of the Book of Isaiah is largely accepted by Biblical scholars. It is also believed by some that Chapter 11, cited above, was written by Deutero-Isaiah. Think it's confusing? That's why Northwestern offered a class.

VAYECHI

WHEREAS WHEN IT CAME TIME TO BLESS HIS SONS, Isaac's eyes were "dim from seeing" (Gen. 27:1), that is, from seeing the disharmony between sons, Jacob's eyes were dim from his own shielding them.

The Torah says of Jacob, at the time of the blessings, "The eyes of Jacob were dim from a beard (מזקן)" (Gen. 48:10). To what was the dimness of his eyes being compared? To the goodness and pleasantness of brothers dwelling together, as it is written, "How good and how pleasant it is that brothers dwell together. It is like fine oil on the head running down onto the beard (הזקן)" (Ps. 133:1–2). Just as one must shield one's eyes to prevent anointing oil poured on the head from running into one's eyes, so, too, did Jacob shield his eyes. But why did Jacob shield his eyes at all? It was because he was afraid that if he looked upon his sons and the sons of Joseph dwelling together in harmony that it would all be an illusion, as he says, "I had never expected to see you again, and here God has let me see your children as well" (Gen. 48:11). He did not think he could see them – because he was shielding his eyes – but he did see them – because God gave him vision through the darkness.

Thus was Jacob able to tell his sons, "Gather yourselves together, that I may tell you that which shall befall you in the end of days" (Gen. 49:1), because he had been granted divine vision.

Notes

This parasha had me in a few directions. The very first sentences say, "Someone told Joseph that his father was sick," and "Someone told Jacob that Joseph had come" (Gen. 48:1-2). But, who? The Torah never says.

Near the end, the Torah states that when Joseph's brothers "saw that their father was dead . . ." (Gen. 50:15). What could they have seen? The verse before they had already buried him!

In between those curiosities was the one I focused on – the dimness of Jacob's eyes. I believe the Torah intentionally contrasts Jacob's eyes with those of Isaac, who was famously blind. Jacob, we are told, was dim "from age (מזקן)." Those familiar with old Jewish men might not be surprised to learn that the Hebrew word for "old age" or "old man" or "elder," "זקן," is the same word for "beard." (See the connection?) Wanting to find some Scriptural hook to explain the dimness of his eyes, I searched and found the passage from Psalms. It was perfect. It referred not only to a "beard," but also to the harmony of brothers dwelling together – a perfect end cap to Jacob's life. The Psalm fit the theme. The only part then was to craft the analogy of the oil that fit the rest of the midrash.

שמות

[*Shemot*]

EXODUS

SHEMOT

"AND IT CAME TO PASS IN THE COURSE OF THOSE MANY days that the king of Egypt died; and the children of Israel sighed (ויאנחו) by reason of the bondage" (Ex. 2: 23). What follows this? God calls to Moses out of the burning bush. But which came first: did Moses have to await the cry of Israel to be called to fulfill his role as redeemer, and then God set about the Exodus; or did Israel need to wait for Moses to be called? The timing in the Torah seems ambiguous, for it says "in the course of those many days," and later "*Now* Moses was keeping the flock (Ex. 3:1)," meaning that these things happened seemingly at the same time.

This is resolved by a later passage, which makes it clear that God was waiting on Israel before He called upon Moses to bring about their redemption. Thus Isaiah says (Isa. 35:10):

> And the ransomed of the LORD shall return,
> And come with shouting to Zion,
> Crowned with joy everlasting.
> They shall attain joy and gladness,
> While sorrow and sighing (ואנחה) flee.

Therefore we are told that when Israel sighed, God remembered his promise to return them to Eretz Yisrael. What is the further proof of this? Because He caused the sighing to flee before it came up to

Him, as it is written, "and the children of Israel sighed *by reason of the bondage*, and they cried, and their cry came up unto God *by reason of the bondage*" (Ex. 2:23). That is, while they sighed and cried, God immediately decreed that they should return to Zion, and the sighing immediately fled.

Notes

The first parasha of Exodus packs Moses' early history into a few meaningful stories, and each leaves the reader wanting and questioning. For example, Moses' mother saw that he was a "good child," and hid him three months. What did she see? Would she have not hidden him had he not been "good?" When Moses murders the Egyptian, he saw that "there was no man." So how did the Israelites hear about it, as mentioned in the next verse?

The main interpretive aspect of Moses' story, however, is his first encounter with God at the burning bush. The Exodus encounters with God are the most mysterious of the Torah. In the books of Leviticus and Numbers, God speaks to Moses from the Tent of Meeting. In the book of Genesis, God speaks in dreams. But in the book of Exodus, God speaks in fundamentally indescribable ways. The multiple accounts of the Sinai experience in Exodus are, like the mountain itself, covered. As Rabbi Heschel famously wrote, the Biblical account of Revelation is itself a midrash.[1]

The question raised by Shemot is this: What was God waiting for to save the Israelites? Was He waiting for Moses to be ready? Or was He waiting for Israel to cry out to Him? The midrash begins from there.

---

1. Heschel, R. Abraham J., *God in Search of Man*, Noonday Press 1955, at p. 185.

VA-AYRA

WHEN GOD SPEAKS TO MOSES JUST BEFORE SEND-ing him to Pharaoh, He states that He established his covenant with Abraham, Isaac and Jacob "to give them the land of Canaan." But then, God adds to the covenant, upon hearing the groaning of the children of Israel due to the bondage ("And moreover, I have heard the groaning . . ." [Ex. 6:5]). Now, He tells Moses to tell the children of Israel, "I will take you to Me for a people (Ex. 6:7) . . . and I will bring you into the land (Ex. 6:8) . . ." The original covenant, of the land, is now twofold: the land and peoplehood.

However, the children of Israel did not embrace this addition to the covenant. This is because the children of Israel were already of a mindset of being enslaved to a master, Pharaoh, and did not want to be enslaved to another master, God. Therefore, the Torah tells us, "they hearkened not unto Moses for impatience of spirit, and for cruel bondage" (Ex. 6:9). That is, they did not embrace the new covenant because their spirit had been crushed by years of bondage.

To what can this be compared? This is like a poor community that receives protection from the king. Because they are poor, they do not recognize the benevolence of the king. They do not know that the king protects them from worse calamities. One day, when the king tells them that if they express loyalty to him, he will protect them forever and enrich them, they respond, "We have always been loyal, and what has it gotten us?" So the king shows them other communities that the king has conquered, where the subjects defied him, and those communities were far worse off. And so the people expressed loyalty to the king and were rewarded.

So it is with God and the children of Israel. As long as they were enslaved in Egypt, they were not ready to accept the mantle of God's peoplehood. But when God demonstrated His power and protection, through the plagues brought upon Egypt, the people accepted the entire covenant.

This is also what is meant by the hardening of Pharaoh's heart. After one plague, Pharaoh would have let the Israelites leave. But God had not yet convinced the Israelites of His power and majesty. Therefore, God continually hardened Pharaoh's heart so that additional plagues would be brought. The plagues were meant to demonstrate God's power to Israel, even more than to the Egyptians.

Notes

The notion that the plagues were for the Israelites rather than to convince Pharaoh is not new, though I had never considered it before this midrash and only found it in other sources later.

Originally I had tried to make sense of the plagues. In plagues 1–3, Aaron is the principal actor. In plagues 4 and 5, Moses speaks, and God does. In plague 6, God tells Moses and Aaron jointly, but Moses acts alone to bring it about. In plagues 7-9, Moses announces the plagues himself. And, in plague 10, God acts alone.

I couldn't really find a meaningful pattern.

The natural place to begin anyway was the idea of the covenant. The covenant (or covenants) between God and Israel in the Torah are central to the Jewish religion. The fact that this portion, for the first time in the Torah, suggests a benefit of the covenant would be being "God's people" as opposed to merely having possession of the land, was incredibly significant. The idea of God's chosen people plays itself out for the rest of the Torah. It was born in this parasha. The plagues explain how God convinced them.

BO

WHAT IS THE NATURE OF THE NINTH PLAGUE, DARK-ness "which may be felt (ימש)" (Ex. 10:21)? It is like the primordial darkness of the first three days of Creation, before God created the residents of the firmament: the sun, the moon, the stars and the angels on the fourth day. This is why the darkness lasted for only three days (Ex. 10:22).

What was so significant about this darkness? It was spiritual darkness because there were no angels to intercede on behalf of the living creatures. When man began to sin, his repentance would bring the angels to intercede on his behalf. But when his repentance was insincere, it was as if there had been no angels to intercede, and repentance would bring him no merit. In this way, repentance without the heavenly angels is like the repentance of Pharaoh, who was the first to repent to God (Ex. 10:17), but was spiritually dark and therefore his repentance brought him no merit. How is this shown? Because Pharaoh's plea, "Forgive, I pray thee (שא נא = 352)" (Ex. 10:17) was lacking "4" from the darkness that ensued (= ימש 356). His repentance did not bring him the light (i.e., the angels) of the fourth day.

Notes

This one popped out at me almost immediately. The thing I found remarkable about this parasha is that Pharaoh – the evil Pharaoh – is the first person in the Torah to actually repent and seek forgiveness from God. One would think he would be credited for that, but nothing really comes of it. The Torah doesn't seem to comment on it one way or another. It just happens.

To understand what was going on, I mapped out Pharaoh's statement (Ex. 10:16–17):

a)   *Calls Aaron and Moses in haste* – וימהר

b)   *"I have sinned"* – חטאתי

c)   *"Now"* – ועתה

d)   *"Therefore"* – שא

e)   *"Pray thee"* – נא

f)   *"I have sinned"* – חטאתי

g)   *"Forgive me only this one time"* – אך הפעם

I also notice the odd phrase, "darkness which may be felt (וימש)" (Ex. 10:21). Doing the gematria, the Hebrew word in the latter phrase totaled 356, whereas the heart of Pharaoh's statement, "Therefore, I pray thee (שא נא)" totaled 352. The difference, 4, related to darkness from the Creation story – the fourth day is when the sun, moon, stars, and (according to other midrashim) angels were created.

BESHALACH

AT THE RED SEA, THE TORAH TELLS: "And the angel of God, who went before the camp of Israel, removed and went behind them; and the pillar of cloud removed from before them, and stood behind them; and it came between the camp of Egypt and the camp of Israel; and there was the cloud and the darkness and it cast a light upon the night and the one came not near the other all the night" (Ex. 14:19–20).

How is this passage to be interpreted?

"*And the angel of God*," – this is an angel of judgment, as the use of "God" instead of "LORD" indicates judgment over mercy – "*who went before the camp of Israel, removed and went behind them; and the pillar of cloud removed from before them, and stood behind them; and it*" – the cloud – "*came between the camp of Egypt and the camp of Israel; and there was the cloud and the darkness*" – because the angel of God had departed, leaving the cloud and darkness – "*and it*" – the cloud – "*cast a light upon the night*" – because God had sent an angel of mercy to transfer the LORD's light to the cloud – "*and the one came not near the other all the night*" – the angel of judgment stayed away from Israel.

How is it shown that God's light could be transferred from one entity to another in times when the LORD desires to show mercy upon Israel? As the prophet Isaiah relates (Isa. 60:19-22):

No longer shall you need the sun for light by day, nor the shining of the moon for radiance by night; for the LORD shall be your light everlasting, your God shall be your glory. Your sun shall set no more, Your moon no more withdraw; For the LORD shall be a light to you forever . . . And your people, all of them righteous, shall possess the land for all time . . . The smallest shall become a clan; the least, a mighty nation. I the LORD will speed it in due time.

So it was with Israel at the Red Sea. Though they cried out against God (Ex. 14:12), and the angel of judgment was prepared to execute judgment against them, the LORD remembered His commitment to make them a mighty nation, and sent the angel of mercy to be their salvation, and to light up the night with His light as an indication of His mercy.

Notes

The chaos of the flight from Egypt showed itself in all the different possible items I considered. The Torah states the children of Israel went up "armed (וחמשים)" out of the land. I loved the possibility that they may have left "armed" with חמשים (i.e., Chumashim, the Hebrew word[1] for the Five Books of Moses – the Torah!). Moses was also instructed to tell Israel that Pharaoh would change his mind and follow after them (Ex. 14:4), so why were they so distraught and surprised when it actually happened (Ex. 14:11)? There is also an interesting bit about Shabbat. God had not commanded Israel about Shabbat (this was pre-Sinai). It is not surprising then that God instructs Moses that he will rain bread on Israel, and the

---

1. From the Hebrew word for the number 5, חמש.

people will "gather a certain portion every day" (Ex. 15:4). On the sixth day, however, they are told to gather a double portion (Ex. 15:5). This is clearly in anticipation of Shabbat, except they aren't told not to gather on the seventh day. In fact, just prior, they were told to gather "every day." Did Moses already know about Shabbat so he could explain this?

While all of that was well and good, the truly confounding part of this parasha was the passage about the cloud and the angels at the banks of the Red Sea. It seemed to move up and back, forward, then behind, in light then in darkness. Where was it really? And why? There was a cloud, and there was light, and the cloud seemed to cast a light, but they "came not near each other." It occurred to me that the light must be transferred, somehow. Searching for passages about light, I came upon the passage of Isaiah quoted in the midrash.

YITRO

"Now Mount Sinai was altogether on smoke, because the Lord *descended* upon it in fire" (Ex. 19:18). "And the Lord said unto Moses: 'Lo, I *come* unto thee in a thick cloud, that the people may hear when I speak with thee'" (Ex. 19:9).

"And the Lord said unto Moses . . . 'the Lord *will come down* in the sight of all the people'" (Ex. 19:11).

The Torah's retelling of Revelation tells of three Revelations: the Revelation of the past, the Revelation of the present, and the Revelation of the future. What is the nature of these Revelations?

The Revelation of the past: Here the Lord descended in fire and spoke only to Moses, as it is written, "And when the voice of the horn waxes louder and louder, Moses spoke, and God answered him by a voice" (Ex. 19:19). But God's Revelation in the fire was imperfect, for God descended in a fire and needed to communicate in a voice, as it is stated, "But the Lord was not in the fire. And after the fire, a still small voice" (I Kings 19:12).

The Revelation of the present: Here the Lord descends in a cloud and spoke to Moses, though the people could hear. This is our current state of Revelation – a Revelation that is obscured, but clarified by the teaching of Moses.

The Revelation of the future: Here the Lord will descend unobscured, without fire or cloud, "in the sight of all the people." This is the Revelation of the World to Come, when our understanding will be perfect and in perfect communion with God. This is the meaning of the promise of Jeremiah (Jer. 31:32–34):

> But such is the covenant I will make with the House of Israel after these days – declares the LORD: I will put my teaching into their inmost being and inscribe it upon their hearts. Then I will be their God, and they shall be My people. No longer will they need to teach one another and say to one another, "Heed the LORD;" for all of them, from the least of them to the greatest, shall heed Me – declares the LORD.

Notes

First of all, that passage from Jeremiah is my favorite passage in Scripture. I was really glad when I was able to use it.

Second, nothing fascinates me more than the Sinai Revelation. Something happened there that was so indescribable, the Torah appears not to even try. If I could go back in time to any point in history, I would put myself at Sinai for Revelation, just to experience it.

With that background, I really focused my attention on what the Torah was saying happened. To no one's surprise, there was no consistent story, even within this Exodus text. God was there. God is there. He descended. He will descend. He was obscured by a cloud. He was in sight of all the people. There was, and is, no real answer to what really happened at Sinai. The Torah seems to preserve many interpretations of the event, perhaps teaching us that each perceived (and continues to perceive) Revelation from God in his or her own way.

In any event, the different passages were mapped out:

a) *Past tense → fire → spoke to Moses*
b) *Present tense → cloud → spoke to Moses, but people could hear*
c) *Future tense → no fire, no cloud → full sight of the people*

Once I had that, it was just a matter of finding the right meaning.

MISHPATIM

THE PERFECTION OF THE TORAH IS PRESERVED through its having been written down, for the Torah itself teaches that a purely oral tradition may be adhered to, but unless it is in writing, its teachings can be doubted, or lost through carelessness or misinterpretation.

It is written twice that when Moses tells the people God's laws, they respond in unison, "We will do (נעשה)" (Ex. 24:3, Ex. 19:8). However, when Moses reads the laws to them from a book, the people respond, "We will do (נעשה), and obey (ונשמע)" (Ex. 24:7). What is the reason for "and obey (ונשמע)," since it is hardly different from the commitment to "do?" Read it not as "and obey (ונשמע)," but instead "and it was heard (ונשמע)."

What was heard? It was direct Revelation from the voice of God, as it is written, "The sound of the cherubs' wings could be heard (נשמע) as far as the outer court, like the voice of El Shaddai when He speaks" (Ezek. 10:5). Further, Scripture tells us that such words are perfect, saying, "There is no utterance, there are no words, whose sound goes unheard (נשמע) . . . the teachings of the LORD are perfect . . . the decrees of the LORD are enduring . . . the precepts of the LORD are just . . . the instruction of the LORD is lucid" (Ps. 19:4–9).

Thus it is that when the people heard the teachings from the book, instead of through an oral tradition, they knew that the teaching was "perfect," "enduring," "just" and "lucid."

Notes

These kinds of parashot are the most challenging to write midrash on. They are dense with law code (this is, after all, the beginning of the "law-giving" in the Torah). At least in Exodus (unlike Leviticus, which had all of those same difficulties), the language is grander, more mysterious and allusive. The godly quality in the book of Leviticus, is that of Holiness. In the book of Exodus, it is fiery, all-powerful and awesome Revelation. Thus, here, God doesn't just promise to destroy those guilty of idolatry, but says they shall be "utterly destroyed" (Ex. 22:19). That linguistic flourish, of not just destruction but "utter destruction" might require some explanation.

The passage that caught my eye, however, was the people's response to Revelation: we will do, and we will obey. That response is a trove of midrashic interpretation. Here I tried to find my own meaning.

The thing that I hadn't seen addressed in prior midrashim was the association of "doing" and "obeying" with the source. In 24:3, Moses told the people the laws, and they responded, "we will do." In 24:7, he read them from the "Book of the Covenant" (this itself is entirely mysterious – what was this book and where did it go?), and they respond "we will do and obey." The different sources, the oral and the written, immediately called to mind the different Torahs in Judaism – the Written Torah (i.e., the Torah consisting of the Five Books of Moses) and the Oral Torah (i.e., the Mishnah and Talmuds). The tension between Written and Oral Torah is built into the fabric of Judaism (at least since the destruction of the Second Temple in 70 C.E. and the emergence of the rabbinic model of Judaism). That this passage might shed light on a response to written and oral Torah was too tantalizing to ignore. Searching the word for "obey (ונשמע)" provided the Scriptural context in Psalms and Ezekiel to complete the midrash.

TERUMAH

NTIL THE CHILDREN OF ISRAEL'S GREAT SIN OF THE Golden Calf, God did not require the sacrifice of animals. The only sacrifice God required of Israel was enough to make the loaves of the showbread for the Tabernacle. These loaves were to be enough to be a sign between God and Israel that his covenant would be everlasting. This is inferred from what God explained about his meeting with Moses from above the Ark of the Covenant, saying He would speak, "all things which *I will give thee in commandment* (אצוה אותך) unto the children of Israel" (Ex. 25:22).

How do we infer that this really refers to the loaves of the showbread? Because we may read "אצוה אותך" as "batches of loaves (אצוה) are your sign (אותך)" – for following this passage, the Torah tells of the instructions for the showbread, "And thou shalt set upon the table showbread before Me always" (Ex. 25:30). The Torah later makes clear that this refers to multiple batches of loaves (Lev. 24:6), and that it shall commemorate Shabbat "as an everlasting covenant" (Lev. 24:8).

We can also infer from connection between this passage and Jeremiah that the only offering sought by God was for the showbread. It is written first, "Speak unto the children of Israel, that they take for Me an offering; *of every man whose heart maketh him willing ye shall take My offering*" (Ex. 25:2). This passage immediately precedes the passage about the showbread. Thus, the sacrifices of animals were not originally decreed. This is confirmed by Jeremiah, as it is written, "For when I freed your fathers from the land of Egypt, I did not speak with them or command them concerning burnt offerings or sacrifice. But this is what I commanded them: Do My bidding, that I may be your God and you may be My people; walk only in the way that I enjoin upon you (אצוה), that it may go well with you" (Jer. 7:22–23).

Notes

This one took a little creativity with language and letters. I began by trying to explore what the Torah meant by "all things which I will give thee in commandment." The phrase seemed awkward and sent me right to the Hebrew. The Hebrew words were "אצוה אותך." I hadn't encountered the word "אצוה" before, but I recognized a root in the word "אותך," namely, "אות," or "sign."[1] The addition of the "ך" as a suffix would, grammatically, change the word to a possessive, i.e., "your sign."

Having that as the foundation, the next step was to find what the "sign" was. I looked up the other word, "אצוה," and I found that it could refer to "batches." (The proper spelling for "batches" would have probably been "אצווה," but it was close enough to take some liberties). That discovery was stunning, because just after that passage was the instruction about the showbreads, literally, "batches" of loaves.

---

1. Shabbat, for example, is referred to as a "sign . . . for all time" in a famous passage in Exodus that is repeated as part of the Shabbat Amidah, ("ביני ובין בני ישראל אות הוא לעולם", "It [Shabbat] is a sign between me and the people of Israel for all time") (Ex. 31:17). Similarly, the Shema prayer refers to the tefillin as a "sign" (Deut. 6:8). ("וקשרתם לאות על ידך," "And you shall bind them as a sign upon your hand."). This is why tefillin are not worn on Shabbat; the sign of tefillin is not necessary because Shabbat is itself a sign.

Having in hand that the showbread loaves would be a sign, I still didn't know what to do with that. But, searching Scripture for the word "אצוה" led me to the passage in Jeremiah that not only talked about the immediate aftermath of leaving Egypt (so temporally applied to this parasha), but also made the connection with sacrifices.

TETZAVEH

HOW MUCH DOES THE PRIESTHOOD OWE TO MOSES? When God sought to transmit the Torah to Israel, and to make them a "kingdom of priests" (Ex. 19:6), God summoned to Mount Sinai (1) Moses, (2) Aaron, (3) Nadab and Abihu, and (4) the 70 elders (Ex. 24:9). But Moses foresaw that Nadab and Abihu would die, and the chain of priesthood would be broken. When he raised this to God, God began to delineate the priesthood by instructing, "And bring near unto thee (1) thou (i.e., Moses), (2) Aaron thy brother, (3) and his sons with him from (4) among the children of Israel" (Ex. 28:1). But Moses was again concerned. First, Nadab and Abihu could not perpetuate the priestly line because of their death, and Aaron's other sons, Eleazar and Ithamar only served "in the presence of Aaron their father" (Num. 3:4), so that the "children of Israel" would be left without a line of priests after Aaron. So again, God clarified, "even (1) Aaron, (2) Nadab and Abihu, (3) Eleazar and Ithamar, (4) the sons of Aaron" (Ex. 28:1). And finally Moses was content, that although he was excluded from the priesthood, the chain of succession was made clear.

Notes

I actually wrote this one and Shemini (the parasha from Leviticus involving the death of Nadab and Abihu) at the same time. Nadab and Abihu were mentioned by name here, and then figured prominently later when they attempted to kindle a fire in the Tabernacle and were immediately struck dead by God. This was one of the rare cases where I couldn't choose just one midrash to write, so wrote one for this parasha and one for Shemini.[1]

The first verse of Chapter 28 is repetitive. It reads:

And take to you Aaron your brother, and his sons with him, from among the people of Israel, that he may minister to me in the priest's office, Aaron, Nadab and Abihu, Eleazar and Ithamar, Aaron's sons.

Reading that, it wasn't clear who was taken to whom, nor why. And why did Eleazar and Ithamar show up in the second half of the sentence, grouped separately from Nadab and Abihu? Nadab and Abihu had already been mentioned previously. They had been among those that went up into Mount Sinai with Moses with Aaron and the elders (Ex. 24:9).

So, we had three groupings of four mentioned:

Group A (Ex. 24:9)	Group B (Ex. 28:1)	Group C (Ex. 28:1)
Moses	You (Moses)	Aaron
Aaron	Aaron your brother	Nadab and Abihu
Nadab and Abihu	His sons	Eleazar and Ithamar
70 elders	Children of Israel	Aaron's sons

This looked more and more like a chronological delineation of the priesthood. What brought it together was the reference in Numbers 3:4 that Eleazar and Ithamar served in the presence of Aaron.

---

1. See commentary on Shemini.

KI-TISSA

THE EPISODE OF THE GOLDEN CALF CAME ABOUT BE-
cause of the people's persistent fear, jealousy and distrust of
Moses. The Torah relates, "And when the people saw that
Moses delayed to come down (כי בשש משה לרדת) from the mount,"
they asked Aaron to build them an idol (Ex. 32:1). But what was
it that "the people saw," given that it was the fact that Moses had
disappeared altogether that gave rise to their anxiety?

We should read not "Moses delayed to come down (כי בשש משה
לרדת)," but "And when the people saw that Moses was with Six (בשש)
to come down." To what did the "Six" refer? Scripture tells us, "Six
things the LORD hates" (Prov. 6:16). Each of the Six relates to an
episode in the life of Moses that caused a negative reaction among
the people, so that what the people saw in Moses at that time was a
man whom they feared, were jealous of and distrusted, and therefore they sought to replace him with an idol:

Proverbs 6:16	Refers to:
An arrogant look	The people's fear of Moses's face: "And all the children of Israel saw Moses, behold, the skin of his face sent forth beams; and they were afraid to come nigh to him" (Ex. 34:30).
A lying tongue	The people not believing Moses because of his uncircumcised lips: "And Moses spoke before the LORD saying, 'Behold, the children of Israel have

Proverbs 6:16	Refers to:
	not hearkened unto me . . . who am of uncircumcised lips'" (Ex. 6:12).
Hands that shed innocent blood	The people's accusation that he killed an innocent Egyptian: "And he said: 'Thinkest thou to kill me, as thou didst kill the Egyptian?'" (Ex. 2:14).
A heart that plots wicked plans	The people's accusation that he brought them to the wilderness to die: "Why have you brought us up out of Egypt, to kill us and our children and our cattle with thirst" (Ex. 17:3)?
A false witness who speaks lies	The perception that Moses had broken the just-made covenant with God: "And he cast the tablets out of his hands, and broke them beneath the mount" (Ex. 32:19).
He who sows discord among brothers	The jealousy over having set Moses and Aaron over the other members of the tribe of Levi: "Ye take too much upon you, seeing all the congregation are holy, every one of them, and the LORD is among them; wherefore then lift ye up yourselves above the assembly of the LORD" (Num. 16:6)?

Notes

*I don't know if there is a word in Biblical Hebrew for "notice," or "recognize" beyond the word, "*ירא*," which means "see." But here, the Torah uses that word to say that the people "saw" that Moses had not come down. "Seeing" implies an actual sight of something, whereas here it was clear that what they "saw" was an absence of something. I looked hard at the language. Did Moses begin his descent in their presence and then stop? Nothing suggested that. Was he visible on the mountain the whole time, and they just saw that he stayed up there? Perhaps.*

*The other linguistic clue was the use of the words "*כי בשש*" to say "was delayed." The word "*שש*" (sheish) is the Hebrew word for "six." The prefix*

"ב" in Hebrew means "in" or "with." So, literally, the word "בשש" could be read as "with six," as in, the people saw Moses was "with six."

The number six has many possible meanings in Judaism: the directions in space (up, down, north, south, east and west) used to signify the presence of God everywhere (this is reflected in the directions in which Jews shake the lulav and etrog on Sukkot); the days of the week prior to Shabbat; the fact that the cloud covered Sinai for six days, and on the seventh day Moses went in (Ex. 24:16); the seraphim in Isaiah's vision (Isa. 6:1) had six wings; and other Kabbalistic meanings (e.g., the six middle Sefirot).

When I searched for "six," I found the passage in Proverbs of the "six things the LORD hates." Given that the delay would lead to the most hateful sin imaginable by the Jewish people (the Golden Calf), the passage from Proverbs thematically fit. At that point, it was a matter of scouring Scripture to relate each of those six things to an episode in the life of Moses. As so often happens, I was shocked at how well it lined up.

VAYAKHEL

W HY WAS BEZALEL CHOSEN TO BUILD THE Tabernacle?

The Shechinah (שכינה) asked, "Who will build me a holy dwelling place (משכן) from among those made in the image of God (בצלם אל)?"

The LORD said, "All you need is a מ! Bezalel (בצלאל) will give you his, so that the image of God shall be called by name בצלאל," (as it is written, "See, the LORD has called by name Bezalel (בצלאל)" [Ex. 35:30]), "and you shall have the Tabernacle (המשכן)."

When Bezalel protested that his "mem" (מ/ם)[1] was being taken from him, and so his name would no longer refer to the image of God (בצלם אל), God reassured him that what was taken will be replaced and then some, as it is written, "He hath filled him with the spirit of God, in wisdom, in understanding, and in knowledge" (Ex. 35:31).

---

1. Like many Hebrew letters, the letter mem [ם/מ] has two forms: one that is only used at the end of a word [ם], and one when used anywhere else in a word [מ].

Notes

This one was pretty obvious. The name Bezalel (בצלאל) was almost certainly written with the intention to call to mind the narrative from the Creation story of making man "in the image (בצלם)" of God (אל). The midrashic piece was simply manipulating the letters to figure out what to do with the "ם" of "בצלם" to get to "בצל אל." That answer came from the word for the Tabernacle, "משכן," which comes from the root "שכן," to dwell. The Tabernacle is a dwelling place for God's presence, also referred to as the "Shechinah (שכינה)," which comes from the same root, "שכן."

PEKUDEY

"AND HE REARED UP THE COURT ROUND ABOUT THE Tabernacle and the altar, and set up the screen of the gate of the court. *So Moses finished the work*" (Ex. 40:33).

Of all other activities in setting up the Tabernacle, Moses' actions conclude with, "as the LORD commanded Moses" (Ex. 40:19, 21, 23, 25, 27, 29, 32). Here instead, the Torah says not "as the LORD commanded Moses," but "So Moses finished the work." This is because Moses had finished the work prematurely, and contrary to God's commandment. Indeed, after setting up the court round about, and setting up the screen of the gate of the court, Moses is further commanded to "take the anointing oil, and anoint the Tabernacle, and all that is therein . . . and it shall be holy" (Ex. 40:9).

Why did Moses leave off the work when he did? This was out of courtesy to God, to let God finish the construction of the Tabernacle Himself, since it was to be the abode of His glory. When it came time to anoint the Tabernacle, Moses said to God, "Should I anoint this place, where Your glory will reside? When a man anoints a person or a thing to You, the anointed is still an instrument of a human master. But the Tabernacle will be Your instrument entirely, not subject to any human master. Therefore, You, God, should anoint it Yourself. Only then can Torah emanate from it. Thus it is written of the Torah, 'Because the LORD has anointed me; He has sent me as a herald of joy to the humble, to bind up the wounded of heart, to proclaim release to the captives, liberation to the imprisoned; To proclaim a year of the LORD's favor and a day of vindication by our God; To comfort all who mourn.' (Isa. 61:1–2). What can do all those things besides Your Torah, which You shall speak to me from the Tabernacle?" And God replied, "You have spoken well, Moses." Thus, "And the glory of the LORD filled the Tabernacle" (Ex. 40:35).

Notes

This one was really laborious, but I liked how it turned out. It is one of the first ones where I experimented with writing a "story" to explain something between the lines. Midrashic literature is full of these kinds of exchanges created out of the commentator's imagination to explain Torah. (Rashi's recasting of God's instruction to Abraham concerning the binding of Isaac into a conversation is a well-known example).[1]

What I ended up with was a long way from where I started.

The passage I spent the most time on turned out to be a dead end. I had focused on a very detailed passage about the Tabernacle, 38:21, which read, "This is the sum of the things of the tabernacle, of the tabernacle of Testimony, as it was counted, according to the commandment of Moses, for the service of the Levites, by the hand of Ithamar, son to Aaron the priest." That laundry list of pairings of people and things (Tabernacle/testimony, commandment/Moses, service/Levites, hand/Ithamar, son/Aaron or Aaron/priest) must have meant something. The $5 \times 2 = 10$ might have been any number of things. I played with the first letters of each pairings and put them in every combination I could to see if I could find a useful acronym. Nothing. So I moved on.

---

1. Gen. 22:2: "Take now your son," [Abraham: Which son? I have two.] "Your only son," [Abraham: Each is the only son of his mother.] "Whom you love," [Abraham: I love them both.] "Isaac."

Another of the linguistic curiosities here was the contrast between the commandment to Moses to "set up (ושמת)" the court around Tabernacle (Ex. 40:8) and the later statement that he "erected (ויקם)" it (Ex. 40:33). I spent hours with those two words. I calculated all kinds of values using gematria. I found the difference between them (590) and spent hours searching the dictionary for words that added up to 590. Nothing there either.

Finally, I also noted that Moses "finished the work," but it did not say "as the LORD commanded Moses" as in all the other verses. What I found to be the most interesting thing here was the fact that, while "Moses finished the work," the Torah does not say that he had anointed the Tabernacle as he was instructed to do in verse 9 ("and you shall take the anointing oil and anoint the Tabernacle"). It looked like he had finished early. If he had, that would explain why the Torah did not say "as the LORD commanded Moses;" he had not actually followed the commandment to finish when he did. The passage from Isaiah helped frame the conversation I wrote to explain all of this.

וִיקְרָא

(Vayikra)

LEVITICUS

VAYIKRA

THE TORAH TELLS OF THREE TYPES OF SIN OFFERINGS required: one for the priests, one for the rulers and the whole congregation, and one for the common people. This is to teach us how God regards the sins of each.

Of all three types, the sin offering is required when any of them do "that which should not be done (אשר לא תעשינה)" (Lev. 4:2, 13, 22, 27). This is to teach that God commanded all three groups identically.

However, their sins are recited differently.

Of the priests, it is said that a sin offering is required if they commit a sin "of all the commandments (מכל מצות)" (Lev. 4:2). This is to teach that the priests were held to the highest standard – they were to obey all the laws, those applying to the common people as well as those applying only to the priests.

Of the rulers and the whole congregation, it is said that a sin offering is required if they commit a sin in any "one of all the commandments (אחת מכל מצות)" (Lev. 4:13, 22). This is to show that when a ruler sins, it is as if the whole congregation had sinned, as it is "one for all (אחת מכל)."

Of the common people, it is said that a sin offering is required if they commit a sin in "one of the commandments (אחת ממצות)" (Lev. 4:27). This is to show that when the common among the people sin, and every time they sin, it will nevertheless be treated by God as their first and only sin.

Notes

Leviticus was a tedious book to write midrash for. In Genesis, Exodus and Numbers, things happen. Leviticus is almost totally law code. It's not necessarily that the midrash is harder; but the book is, well, boring by comparison. Nevertheless, the Project dictated that I plow through . . .

The sacrificial cult is full of rules, most of which make very little sense (especially to the modern Jew). For example, a burnt offering could only be a male, a sin offering could only be a female, but a peace offering could be either. Why does one remove the fat from a peace offering, but not a burnt offering? The Torah makes a distinction between a sin offering and a guilt offering, with the guilt offering being required when one sinned without knowing. How would he know to bring an offering then? And, there are sins of commission, but also sins of omission. Yet the sin offering is only for sins of commission, i.e., "doing things that should not be done" (Lev. 4:2).

It was the different formulations of the sin offering that most intrigued me. Once I mapped out the different sin offerings and the different audiences for each, it was clear that distinctions were being drawn. The midrash explains those distinctions.

TZAV

T HE TORAH TELLS OF THE DIFFERENT STAGES RELATING
to the carrying out of sacrifices. For each of the meal offering, the sin offering and the burnt offering, the Torah
relates that some aspect is "most holy." Specifically:

- Of the "meal offering" it is written, "I have given it [the offering itself] as their portion of My offerings made by fire, it [the
  offering itself] is most holy" (Lev. 6:10).
- Of the "sin offering" it is written, "in the place where the
  burnt offering is killed shall the sin offering be killed before
  the LORD; it [the place] is most holy" (Lev. 6:18).
- Of the "guilt offering" it is written, "And this is the law of the
  guilt offering; it [the law] is most holy" (Lev. 7:1).
- Further of the "guilt offering" it is written, "it shall be eaten in
  a holy place; it [the place] is most holy" (Lev. 7:6).

The order of these commandments reflects the historical order of
the sacrificial laws.

First, the offering itself was sufficient and was holy. These were
like the offerings made by Abraham, before God had designated a
place for sacrifice.

Next in time, sacrifice was made holy though the place where it
was designated: the Tabernacle, and later the Temple.

Next in time, after the Temple was destroyed, sacrifice was made holy by our study of the laws of sacrifice.

In the Time to Come, the Temple will be rebuilt, and sacrifice will be holy again by virtue of the holy place.

Notes

Similar to parasha Vayikra, the Torah differs in its characterizations of the different offerings. In this case, the characterizations had to do with two related concepts: place and holiness. This was another example of mapping out the passages leading to a very elegant and surprisingly consistent midrash.

SHEMINI

"THE WICKED SHALL BE *SILENT* IN *DARKNESS*" (I Sam. 2:7).
To what does this relate? Nadab and Abihu thought that they could combat wickedness by ridding the Tabernacle of darkness, and so they kindled a "strange fire before the Lord" (Lev. 10:1). However, the fire, even if well-intentioned, was not enough to save them. Nadab and Abihu had addressed the darkness, but not the silence.

To prevent death, they had forgotten that they needed to make their voices heard in praise of God, as both silence *and* darkness were necessary for the wicked, as God had warned, "And his voice (קולו) shall be heard going in unto the holy place before the Lord, and coming out, and he will not die" (Ex. 28:35). To what did this voice (קול) refer? To "The voice (קול) of mirth and gladness, the voice (קול) of bridegroom and bride, the voice (קול) of those who cry, 'Give thanks to the Lord of Hosts, for the Lord is good, for his kindness is everlasting!' as they bring thanksgiving offerings to the House of the Lord" (Jer. 33:11).

Notes

As I noted above, this parasha came about as I was working on parasha Tetzaveh,[1] which also mentioned Nadab and Abihu. For that parasha, I was primarily concerned with how and why Nadab and Abihu were mentioned as they were, so naturally I turned forward to this parasha discussing their death.

While Nadab's and Abihu's death was the result of the kindling of a "strange fire," the Torah is notably ambivalent about this. They had died for their action, but the Torah does not suggest that they were evil or had an improper purpose. The ambivalence of the Torah towards their demise suggests that perhaps they were well-intentioned, but overzealous. In Tetzaveh, there is a passage that states, "And it shall be upon Aaron to minister; and his sound shall be heard when he goes in to the holy place before the Lord, and when he comes out, that he should not die." (Ex. 28:35). That raised the possibility that, rather than the "strange fire," their death had to do with not making the proper sound, as Aaron needed to make a sound to avoid dying himself.

The passage from Samuel connected the sound and the strange fire by saying, "The wicked shall be silent in darkness" (I Sam. 2:7). That passage, together with the passage from Jeremiah, provided the link to complete the midrash.

---

1. See commentary on Tetzaveh.

TAZRIA

THE TORAH PROVIDES FOR DIFFERENT PERIODS OF purification for the mother after the birth of a son and after the birth of a daughter.

In the case of a boy, the Torah states that "she shall be unclean seven days; as in the days of the impurity of her sickness shall she be unclean. And in the eighth day the flesh of his foreskin shall be circumcised. And she shall continue in the blood of purification (בדמי טהרה) three and thirty days" (Lev. 12:2–4). So the question is whether "she shall continue in the blood of purification (בדמי טהרה)" thirty-three days beginning after the seven unclean days, for 40 days, or after the eighth day, for 41 days. The better answer is that the period is 40 days, as follows.

In the case of a girl, the Torah similarly states she shall be "unclean two weeks, as in her impurity; and she shall continue in the blood of her purification (טהרה על דמי) sixty-six days" (Lev. 12:5). So in the case of a girl, the period is a total of 80 days. What accounts for the difference? It is clear that the difference in the periods is interrupted by the instructions concerning the circumcision on the eighth day for the boy, which has seemingly nothing to do with the purity of the mother. How then is the act of circumcision of the son sufficient to cut the "blood of purification" in half by 40 days (and not by 39 days if one were to count starting after the eighth day)?

It is written, "A bridegroom of blood (חתן דמים) in regard of the

circumcision" (Ex. 4:26). The extra ם indicates the plural for blood,
דמים. This refers to an additional 40 (ם) days of the blood (דמי) of
purification. Therefore, the woman need only spend 40 days in
the blood of purification when giving birth to a boy, because the
circumcision is credited to her as 40 additional days of purification.

Notes

*I have a certain amount of selfish pride in this one. In his Chumash, Rabbi
Hertz notes, "There is no satisfactory explanation for why the period is
doubled when a female child is born."[1] I guess I showed him!*

---

1. *The Pentateuch and Haftorahs*, Rabbi J.H. Hertz, ed.; Soncino Press (2nd ed., 1960),
page 460.

METZORA

WHY IS THE TORAH SO CONCERNED WITH THE plague of leprosy in defining cleanliness and uncleanliness? Why should superficial blemishes render something unclean, without regard to spiritual blemishes?

This is to teach us that our state of cleanliness is linked to our renewal of spirit. The Torah teaches this by focusing on the skin, which is always in a continual state of renewal. The support for this is found in the difference between "clean" and "unclean," i.e., "to teach when it is unclean (הטמא), and when it is clean (הטהר); this is the law of leprosy" (Lev. 14:57). The difference between "unclean (הטמא)" and "clean (הטהר)" is 164. This evokes the following passage (Lam. 5:21):

> Take us back, O LORD, to Yourself
> And let us come back;
> Renew our days *as of old* (164 = כקדם).

Accordingly, the Torah tells us that "the law of leprosy" is to teach us about the value of renewal, which implies a return to God.

Notes

What I really wish I could have figured out was how the priest was strong enough to wave a lamb and a log for a wave offering (Lev. 14:12).

This midrash is relatively self-explanatory. The question I had is exactly how I framed it, "Why is the Torah so concerned with superficial blemishes?"

ACHAREI MOT

THE TORAH STATES THAT ON YOM KIPPUR, THE HIGH Priest shall kindle incense, so that "the cloud of the incense covers (וכסה) the ark-cover that is upon the testimony, that he die not" (Lev. 16:13). This passage raises difficult questions: (1) Was the cloud of God's presence really so weak in its intensity that it could truly be covered by a cloud of incense? For we also read, "that he come not at all times into the holy place within the veil, before the ark-cover, that he die not; for I appear in the cloud upon the ark-cover" (Lev. 16:2). (2) Should we read God's appearance in the cloud literally as a physical, instead of metaphorical, appearance of God? For the cloud of incense was indeed a physical cloud. Is the physical needed to conceal (כסה) the metaphorical?

This passage is explained by a further passage: "He holds back the face of His throne (כסה), spreading his cloud over it" (Job 26:9). Here, "throne" is purposely misspelled "כסה" rather than the ordinary "כסא" to emphasize that His throne is concealed. This explains the passage. The appearance of God is "upon" the ark-cover (Lev. 16:2), so that the ark-cover is like His throne. Hence, the cloud of incense "covers the ark-cover" (Lev. 16:13), meaning it is really covering His throne, and not Him, for how could any cloud cover Him, i.e., "His glory [is so great that it] covered (כסה) the Heavens" (Hab. 3:3).

So why should the throne be covered from the view of the High Priest on Yom Kippur? Scripture states, "And in mercy a throne (כסא) was established; and he sat upon it in truthfulness *in the tabernacle of David*, judging, and seeking judgment, and quick to do righteousness" (Isa. 16:5). The sight of the throne might remind the High Priest that the throne of mercy was established *in the tabernacle of David*, but there would be a time before and after the "tabernacle of David" that the people would require His mercy. So as not to frighten the High Priest that His mercy would be reserved for a certain time and place, God instructed him to conceal the throne.

Notes

There were some other passages I considered, but all had something to do with God's presence in and around the Tabernacle.

However, like much of Leviticus, the detailed description of ritual provided a more fertile midrashic ground. Here, the reference to the incense, the cloud, and covering or concealing provided several different avenues. Scripture is full of analogies relating to things being covered, concealed or hidden. This midrash mentions just a few. Others I didn't weave in include Proverbs 12:16 ("A fool's wrath is immediately known; but a clever man conceals his humiliation."); Numbers 22:5 ("Behold, there is a people come out from Egypt; behold, they cover the face of the earth, and they are dwelling opposite me."); Isaiah 29:10 ("For the LORD has poured out upon you the spirit of deep sleep, and has closed your eyes, the prophets; and has covered your heads, the seers."); and Job 23:15–17 ("For God makes my heart faint, and the Almighty terrifies me; Because I was not cut off before the darkness, nor has he covered the darkness from my face.").

KEDOSHIM

WHY WAS THIS TORAH PORTION NOT COMPLETE after 19:2, i.e., the commandment "Ye shall be holy; for I the LORD your God am holy?" Surely that commandment contained the essence of all that followed.

It is because although holiness is natural to God, it is unnatural to man, and so we need direction on how to live a holy life. This portion teaches that a holy life is a commanded life. How is this shown?

The commandments in this portion conclude with "I am the LORD" or "I am the LORD your God." The commandments that conclude with "I am the LORD your God" relate to matters that are common to or for the benefit of all creation (hence the reference to "God," the Creator). The commandments that conclude with "I am the LORD" relate to matters unique to man's situation. Thus:

I am the Lord your God:

"first fruits" (Lev. 19:25)	Fruit was made for all creation
"spirits," i.e., angels (Lev. 19:31)	Angels were made for all creation, before man
Love of "strangers" (Lev. 19:34)	All creatures are naturally strangers upon creation
"Justice" (Lev. 19:36)	צדק is repeated four times in this verse, and the attribute of justice was an aspect of creation

I am the Lord your God:

"Holy" (Lev. 19:2, 20:4)	God, who is before all creation, is holy
Parents and Shabbat (Lev. 19:4)	These are things that are for the benefit of all creation
The corner of the field (Lev. 19:10)	Edible crops were made for all creation

I am the Lord:

No profaning the Name (Lev. 19:12)	God's name was given to man alone
Stumbling blocks (Lev. 19:14)	Only man needs this commandment
Sitting idly by the blood of your neighbor (Lev. 19:16)	The beasts do not have this commandment
"Love thy neighbor" (Lev. 19:18)	Only man has "neighbors"
No tattoos (Lev. 19:21)	Only man needs this commandment
Revere the sanctuary (Lev. 19:30)	Only man needs this commandment
Respect elders (Lev. 19:32)	Only man needs this commandment
All the commandments and statutes (Lev. 19:37, 20:8)	Only man needs this commandment

The final commandments that conclude with "I am the LORD" are the commandments to keep all the commandments (Lev. 19:37) and all the statutes (Lev. 20:8). This demonstrates that, like the commandments mentioned above, the obligation to keep "all" commandments and statutes is a commandment unique to man, because without being commanded, he could not achieve holiness.

Notes

Yet again, Leviticus gives us detail that requires exploration. As with many midrashim, simply making a list of the different commandments and assigning categories revealed an underlying structure.

EMOR

WHEN GOD GIVES MOSES THE LIST OF THE HOLI-
days, some are to be observed for "all generations,"
while for others the Torah is silent in this regard.
Specifically, while the bringing of the omer (Lev. 23:14), Shavuot
(Lev. 23:21), Yom Kippur (Lev. 23:31) and Sukkot (Lev. 23:41) are
commanded to be observed "for all generations," Shabbat, Pesach
and Rosh Hashanah do not have that requirement.

This is to teach us that the bringing of the omer, Shavuot, Yom
Kippur and Sukkot will be observed the same way in the Time to
Come, but Shabbat, Pesach and Rosh Hashanah will not.

Regarding Shabbat, in the Time to Come, every day will be like
Shabbat, as it is written, "tomorrow shall be as this day [Shabbat],
and much more abundant" (Isa. 56:12).

Regarding Pesach, in the Time to Come, the wearing of the tefillin will come to mark the celebration of the holiday, as it is written,
"And it shall be when thy son asketh thee in *time to come*, saying,
'What is this?'" (Ex. 13:14), the question shall refer to tefillin, as it
answers, "And it shall be for a sign upon thy hand, and for frontlets
between thine eyes; for by strength of hand the LORD brought us
forth out of Egypt" (Ex. 13:16).

Regarding Rosh Hashanah, in the Time to Come, forgiveness
will be sought and given for all mankind on Rosh Hashanah, not
just Israel, as it is written, "All mankind comes to You, You who hear

prayer. When all manner of sins overwhelm me, You forgive our iniquities . . . You crown the year with Your bounty" (Ps. 65:3–4, 12).

Notes

This parasha is dominated by the discussion of the festivals. And, while it was interesting to contemplate what the prohibition against shaving the "corners" of one's beard (so could I shave the middle part?) might mean, the primary area for exploration was the festivals.

As with prior Leviticus midrashim, this one followed from putting the text into the categories the Torah provided and then extracting meaning.

BEHAR

GOD SAYS TO THE CHILDREN OF ISRAEL, "YE ARE strangers and settlers with Me" (Lev. 25:23). This is to reinforce the punishment of exile, namely that when they do not obey His laws, they are strangers to the land together, and when they do obey His laws, they are settlers in the land together.

But if God and Israel are together in both exile and in the land, then why does the same portion teach us that at the jubilee, "Ye shall return every man unto his possession (אחזתו)" (Lev. 25:10, 13), for is it not written, "I am their possession (אחזתם)" (Ezek. 44:28)? If they are together in exile, then why does Israel need to return? This teaches that though they are strangers to the land together, at that time God and Israel are also strangers to each other. But because God will never abandon the children of Israel, even when they act like strangers to Him, it is told that it is in the power of man to return to Him when they obey His laws, for example, concerning the jubilee.

Notes

I only had two notes on this parasha: Lev. 25:10, "Ye shall return every man unto his possession," and 25:23, "Ye are strangers and settlers with Me." As it turned out, exploring one led me to the other.

When I found the passage from Ezekiel in relation to "possession," it connected the togetherness of God and Israel, "I am their possession" (Ezek. 44:28). If God is Israel's possession, then what did it mean that, (Lev. 25:10) "Ye shall return every man unto his possession" during the jubilee year? This had to imply a separation of man from his possession, or in this case, a separation between Israel and God. That separation related to the next passage, "Ye are strangers and settlers with Me" (Lev. 25:23). The separation of God and Israel in relation to land (i.e., strangers and settlers suggest a geographic aspect) called to mind the exile of the Jews from Israel.

BECHUKOTAI

OW CAN IT BE PROVEN THAT WHEN THE HUMBLE ARE punished, this assures their place in the World to Come? It is written, "If then perchance their uncircumcised heart be humbled (יכנע), and they then be paid the punishment of their iniquity (עונם), then will I remember My covenant . . ." (Lev. 26:41–42).

When one is humbled only as a result of being punished, such humility is not worthy of God remembering His covenant. When, however, one is first humble (140 = כנע), and then nevertheless still receives punishment (166 = עונם) despite his humility, that punishment comes with the promise of repayment through the mercy of the Holy Name (the letters of which = 26). But when? In the World to Come, seeing as he has already been punished in this world.

Notes

There was quite a bit to unpack in that passage. First, it was possible that an uncircumcised heart could be humbled; normally in Scripture a circumcised heart is a sign of connection with God (as with circumcised lips, and the ordinary circumcision of the male). That an uncircumcised heart could be associated with the covenant was noteworthy.

There was also a temporal aspect to this passage. Humility had to precede punishment for God to remember the covenant. If punishment preceded humility, it seems God would not remember the covenant. This made humility of primary significance in relation to repentance, punishment and forgiveness.

As I would typically do when trying to link two words (here, punishment and humility), I used gematria just to see what would come out.

במדבר

(Bemidbar)

NUMBERS

BEMIDBAR

W HEN GOD COMMANDS MOSES TO COUNT THE
Israelites, why does He immediately specify "Even you
and Aaron" (Num. 1:3) when Moses and Aaron were
undoubtedly included among the Israelites? We should imagine the
following conversation:

The LORD commanded Moses, "Take ye the sum of all the
congregation of the children of Israel" (Num. 1:2). But Moses
interjected, "Can I count the tribe of Judah, for it is written, 'Like
the host (צבא) of heaven which cannot be counted, and the sand of
the sea which cannot be measured, so will I multiply the offspring
of My servant David?'" (Jer. 33:22).

God responded, "That refers only to future offspring. But to
prove that Judah can be counted, you shall count each tribe indi-
vidually, as follows: 'Take ye the sum of all the congregation of
the children of Israel, by their families, by their fathers houses,
according to the number of their names, every male, by their polls;
from twenty years old and upward, all that are able to go forth to war
(צבא) in Israel, ye shall number them by their hosts'" (Num. 1:2–3).

But Moses interjected, "Can I also count the tribe of Levi, for it
is written, 'Like the host (צבא) of heaven which cannot be counted,
and the sand of the sea which cannot be measured, so will I multiply
the offspring of My servant David, and of the Levites who minister

to Me'" (Jer. 33:22). That refers to the Levites in the present tense, and not future offspring.

God responded, "As you have correctly stated, the present Levites and the offspring of David are 'Like the host (צבא) of heaven,' and I have said, 'the LORD will punish the host (צבא) of heaven in heaven and kings of earth on earth.' (Isa. 24:21). The host (צבא) of heaven refers to the present Levites, who are the generation of the wilderness and will not survive, and the kings of earth refer to the offspring of David, who will be deposed by the invading army of Babylon, but both of whom will be innumerable when the Messiah comes."

Moses asked, "Shall every Levite of this generation perish before entering the Land?" God responded, "Even you and Aaron" (Num. 1:3).

Notes

I happened on this midrash in a backwards kind of way. I didn't start with the commandment to count in 1:2. Instead, I focused on the purpose of the count, i.e., for the purpose of going to "war (צבא)." The word used there for "war" is "צבא," which is used throughout Scripture for the word "host," as in Isaiah's formulation, the LORD of Hosts, "Adonai Tz'vaot."

Searching Scripture for that term, "צבא," I came across the passages cited above about the different "hosts" being unable to be counted. That suggested a conflict, and from there I crafted the discussion between God and Moses to resolve it.

NASO

I T HAS BEEN TAUGHT THAT WE SHOULD TRY TO ACT LIKE God, for example, "You shall be holy, for I, the LORD, your God, am holy" (Lev. 19:2). But in at least one way we should not strive to be like God, and that is in regards to jealousy. Concerning jealousy, it is written, "The LORD, whose name (שמו) is Jealousy (קנא), is a jealous God" (Ex. 34:14). But it is also written, "The LORD shall be One, and his name (שמו) One" (Zech. 14:9). Thus, only one (the LORD) is entitled to jealousy.

The Torah, however, seems to approve of jealousy in regards to a husband and his wife. Therefore, the Torah instructs that a jealous husband, who suspects his wife of adultery, though there be no evidence to support it (Num. 5:13), shall subject his wife to the ordeal of bitter waters. At the conclusion of the ordeal, the Torah states, "And the man shall be unpunished (ונקה) from guilt, and that woman shall bear her guilt" (Num. 5:31). But this is outrageous! Is the man really clear from guilt, even if he wrongly accuses his wife? The Prophet, Jeremiah, thus clarifies, "If they who rightly should not drink of the cup must drink of it, are you the one to go unpunished? You shall not go unpunished (נקה תנקה לא תנקה)" (Jer. 49:12)! Why is the word "נקה" repeated? It is to be read not as "נקה," but as "קנא (jealousy)," so that the meaning shall be "If they who rightly should not drink of the cup must drink of it, are you the one to go unpunished? Jealousy shall not go unpunished (נקה קנא לא תנקה)!"

Notes

There was an interesting passage in this parasha, 7:89, that says "And when Moses went into the Tent of Meeting to speak with him, then he heard the voice of one speaking to him from the covering that was upon the ark of testimony, from between the two cherubim; and he spoke to him." This passage suggested Moses walked in on God when God was talking to Himself! Fascinating!

Except I didn't write on that one.

Instead, the ritual of the bitter waters and the jealous husband seemed to contain some kind of moral lesson I wanted to explore. This was especially true since the husband got off relatively easily, even if his accusation was false. We have seen continuously that envy and jealousy are to be avoided; this parasha seemed to go to lengths to validate the husband's jealousy.

The close spelling between "clear (i.e., unpunished) (נקה)" and "jealousy (קנא)" suggested a connection.[1] The Jeremiah text allowed me to arrive at a more acceptable interpretation of the ordeal, namely, that jealousy does not go unpunished.

---

1. The last letter of the Hebrew word for jealousy is an Aleph, א, which is silent. Similarly, the last letter of the word for unpunished is a Hey, ה, which at the end of a word is also silent.

BEHALOTECHA

W HY IS THE TORAH'S DESCRIPTION OF WHEN THE children of Israel would journey and when they would encamp so repetitive? It is repetitive, but with important distinctions. Indeed, the Torah describes it as follows:

- Num. 9:17: when the cloud would lift, they would journey; when the cloud descended, they would encamp
- Num. 9:18: when commanded, they would journey; when commanded they would encamp; when the cloud descended, they would encamp
- Num. 9:19: when the cloud was descended, they would encamp
- Num. 9:20: when the cloud was descended, they would encamp; when commanded, they would journey
- Num. 9:21: when the cloud lifted, they journeyed; when the cloud lifted, they journeyed
- Num. 9:22: when the cloud descended, they encamped; when the cloud lifted they journeyed
- Num. 9:23: when commanded they encamped; when commanded they journeyed

Thus, in the cases of the cloud, on five occasions they encamped, and on four they journeyed. In the cases of the commandment, on two occasions they encamped, and on three they journeyed.

Seven journeys and seven encampments are recounted. But, when the message was conveyed via cloud, it was more likely that they encamped; when the message was conveyed via commandment, it was more likely that they journeyed, as shown in the table below.

	They Encamped	They Journeyed
When Commanded	2 times: Num. 9:18, Num. 9:23	3 times: Num. 9:18, Num. 9:20, Num. 9:23
When the Cloud descended	5 times: Num. 9:17, Num. 9:18, Num. 9:19, Num. 9:20, Num. 9:22	
When the Cloud lifted		4 times: Num. 9:17, Num. 9:21, Num. 9:21, Num. 9:22
Totals:	7	7

So what is the meaning of the distinction between the commandment and the cloud? This was to literally fulfill the promise that God had made to Abraham. With respect to Abraham, his journey commenced with a commandment, but he encamped with a vision, as it is written, "Get thee out of thy country, and from thy kindred, and from thy father's house, unto the land that I will show thee" (Gen. 12:1). So it was with his descendants that they would journey upon a commandment ("Get thee out") and encamp with a vision ("unto the land that I will show thee").

Notes

This is yet another example of the Torah's repetition of events and commandments with slight changes, unrolling into a greater lesson. In this case, it was just a matter of counting each occurrence.

I tried to play with the different numbers I counted – 2, 3, 4, 5, 7 and 7 (7 encampments and 7 journeys), but nothing came of it. It made more sense when I aligned it to the promise made to Abraham in Lech Lecha.

SHELACH LECHA

WHEN GOD COMMANDS MOSES TO SEND THE SPIES to Canaan, it is to fulfill an immediate, unconditional gift of the land, "Send thou men, that they may spy out the land of Canaan, *which I give unto the children of Israel*; of every tribe of their fathers shall ye send a man, every one a prince among them" (Num. 13:2). Note that no mission is given to Moses to give to the spies. However, Moses decides to put the people to a test. Therefore, he gives the spies a mission, specifically, that they should see "what the land is that they dwell in, *whether it is good or bad* (אם רעה)" (Num. 13:19). Surely God would not have given the people a land that is "bad." So what was the purpose of Moses evoking the idea that the land could be "bad (רעה)?"

Moses' words were a warning to the people, to remember the conditions of the covenant between God and the people concerning Israel, as it is written, "If she pleases not (אם רעה) her master, who hath espoused her to himself, then shall he let her be redeemed; to sell her unto a foreign people he shall have no power, seeing he hath dealt deceitfully with her" (Ex. 21:8). Accordingly, if the master (the children of Israel) deals deceitfully with her (the land), and she (the land) does not please her master (the children of Israel), who had been espoused to her (the land) in a commitment worthy of marriage, then he (the children of Israel) shall turn her (the land) over to a foreign people and have no power over her.

This is precisely what God decreed upon hearing the spies' report.

But aren't we told that the spies merely gave a slanderous, i.e., untrue report, in that the Hebrew word used for the spies' report is "דבה," which is translated to "slander?" How do we know that they acted "deceitfully?" The Torah also says that they gave an "evil" slanderous report, namely, "דבה רעה" (Num. 14:37), although the word "רעה" in this context might be seen as repetitive. This is to show that the report was not merely untrue, but that it was known to be untrue by the spies when they delivered it, so that it was truly deceitful. It was the deceitful nature of the report that clinched their sentence that the land would be turned over to foreign people while the generation of the Exodus would wander in the wilderness.

Notes

The thing that jumped out at me was that Moses added to God's command. God merely told Moses to send spies to spy out the land. Moses, however, added that they should report back whether it was "good or bad." Of all the things Moses could have asked the spies to report back on, "good or bad" seemed wildly inappropriate. The premise of the covenant was that God was giving them not just a "good" land, but the best land.

The spies' report added further, both to the language and the intrigue. Instead of giving an "evil" (i.e., "bad") report, they gave a "slanderous" report. So, the commandment went from a general commandment to scout the land, to seeing if it was good or evil, to reporting both evil and slander.

Fortunately, the passage from Exodus used the same phrase as Moses had used with the spies, i.e., "if bad (אם רעה)." That same passage had to do with deceit concerning his wife, which was an apt analogy because the Land of Israel is often thought of in rabbinic and midrashic literature as the Jewish people's betrothed.

KORACH

AFTER THE REBELLION OF KORACH, GOD INSTRUCTS
Eleazar to take "the fire pans (המחתת את)" (Num. 17:2) to
change them into a cover plate for the altar, because they
are holy to God. In the course of the instruction, the phrase "the
fire pans" is repeated two more times, but each time without the
definite article, "ה" (i.e., "the"), though in each time, grammatically,
a definite article would have been required. In fact, each time, the
word for "fire pans" is further altered by adding a "ו," which was
omitted from the first reference. Hence, the repeated words for "the
fire pans" is "את מחתות" (Num. 17:3, 4).

Thus, the first reference is definite, but the second and third references are indefinite. Despite the removal of the "ה," when Eleazar
completes the act, he adds a "ו," representing a net addition to the act
(since 6=ו is greater than 5=ה). What Eleazar added was that the fire
pans should also be a "sign" and a "memorial" to the people relative
to the failed rebellion of Korach.

However, following the completion of Eleazar's task, the people
still murmured against Moses and Aaron (Num. 17:6). This is the
result of the sign that Eleazar had created being indefinite.

In response, God instructs Moses to take "rods" from each of
the tribes, so that the rod of Aaron should bloom and be a "sign"
to the people. Here, there is no definite article (i.e., "ה," or "the"),

associated with the taking of rods (instead referred to as "מטה," Num. 17:17). After seeing this sign, the people show contrition for their sinful ways.

What does this teach us?

In all manner of God's signs to us, they are always indefinite. No sign from God comes with certainty. And yet the story draws a distinction between two types of indefinite signs: one which came with a definite purpose from God but which Eleazar made indefinite by his attempt to convert it to a sign through his own manipulation, i.e., by converting the fire pans to a covering for the altar, and therefore adding to God's purpose (namely, that they be associated with the altar for their holiness) as well as Eleazar's intended purpose of being a sign and a memorial; and a second sign which God designated as a sign all along, and which converted, i.e., bloomed, entirely through the work of God. This teaches us that although God's signs are not definite, we will misinterpret them when we try to manipulate what *is* to fit our notions of what a sign from God *should be*. Signs from God come, but they come "as they are." We must accept the things in our life that we believe to be a sign from God as something indefinite, and susceptible to interpretation, but only through a process of analysis, reflection and internalization, and not through a process of manipulation and converting what "*is*" to what "*should be*."

Notes

This was one of the cases where the Hebrew revealed the oddity. In 17:2, it says, "the fire pans (המחתת)." When it next mentions them in the very next verse, however, it says, "מחתות." In 17:2 the Hebrew included the definite article, "the," represented in Hebrew as the prefix, ה–." But the definite article was gone from the next verse, and the letter "ו" was added (which was the grammatically correct way to write the plural to begin with). So, both words needed explanation.

The midrash evolved by recognizing that ו has a value of six, and ה has a value of five, so that Eleazar had attempted to add something when the ו was added. That followed the story. Moses, by contrast, did exactly what he was commanded to do, and the result was different. The presence and absence of definite articles in relation to the various signs provided context for the lesson.

CHUKAT

HOW MUCH DOES THE LORD VALUE PEACE? HE VALUES peace so much that He would send Aaron to Sheol to make peace among his brethren. From where do we know this? From the narrative of the death of Aaron.

The Torah tells us that the LORD spoke to Moses and Aaron "in" Mount Hor (ההר בהר) rather than "from" Mount Hor (Num. 20:22). God tells Moses that Aaron shall be "gathered to his people (יאסף על עמיו)" (Num. 20:24). Moses is further told to take Aaron and his son, Eleazar, "onto (על)" (not "in") Mount Hor (Num. 20:25). Moses is further commanded to strip Aaron of his priestly vestments, place them on Eleazar, and "Aaron shall be gathered (יאסף) and shall die there" (Num. 20:26). Here, however, it is said only that Aaron "shall be gathered (יאסף)," and not "shall be gathered to his people (יאסף על עמיו)." In response, Moses, Aaron and Eleazar go up to (אל) (not "in") Mount Hor (אל הר ההר) (Num. 20:27). Once there, Moses does as instructed: he strips Aaron of his priestly vestments, places them on Eleazar, and we are told "Aaron died there *in* the top of the mount (ההר בראש)" (Num. 20:28).

Now, if the three of them were *on* the mount, how is it that Aaron died *in* the mount? This is because, at the last moment, God recognized that Aaron the peacemaker could still be of use to God, but he would be of no use if he were to be "gathered to his people." Thus, God gathered Aaron to Himself. This is why the Torah states that

Aaron was merely "gathered" upon his death. Gathered to whom? To God. What is further proof? Because Aaron died *in* the mount, and we are told at the outset that the LORD, Himself, is *in* Mount Hor (Num. 20:22). What purpose did God have for Aaron at that moment? Just prior to the death of Aaron, God had caused the earth to swallow up his brethren, the clan of Korach (Num. 16:32). Korach and his clan, now in Sheol, were still bitter and jealous, and so God took Aaron *into* the earth, where Korach then resided, to make peace among them.

Notes

This parasha is reminiscent of the many parashot I've written about involving mountains. There is confusion everywhere: sometimes the characters are up, sometimes in, sometimes on. The key to figuring them out is to write them out, step by step, paying attention to who is where, and when.

Once I realized that Aaron died in the mountain, I made the connection between that and the prior portion of Korach, referring to Aaron's traditional persona as the peacekeeper among the Jews.

BALAK

THREE DIFFERENT WORDS ARE USED TO REFER TO THE curses requested from Balaam. Initially, Balak asks Balaam to "curse (ארה) me these people" (Num. 22:6). When Balaam asks God what to do, he repeats Balak's request, only with a different word, repeating Balak's request as, "curse (קבה) me them" (Num. 22:11). God responds with yet a third word for "curse," saying, "thou shalt not curse (תאר) the people" (Num. 22:12).

Each of the three words used for "curse" has an alternative meaning. "ארה" can also mean "gather." "קבה" can also mean "chamber" or "tent." And "תאר" can mean a "boundary."

The three words also share similar letters, with the letters ה,ר and א each appearing twice in the combination of the three words, and the letters ב, ת and ק each appearing once.

These words and letter combinations combine to foretell the coming curse brought upon the Israelites by the Moabites, even despite Balaam's failure to articulate a particular curse. Namely, these words and letters play out in what follows, i.e., the harlotry with Moabite women and the act of Pinchas to stop the curse.

Pinchas, we are told, upon hearing of an Israelite man taking a Midianite woman, enters their chamber (הקבה) (Num. 25:8) and stabs them both through the belly. Now, the letters ב, ת and ק can be arranged to read "קבת" (belly), as in Pinchas thrust a spear "through her belly (אל קבתה)" (Num. 25:8), just as the letters can be arranged to read בתק, which is another word for "stab" or "pierce." The remaining letters, ה,ר and א, can be arranged to read ראה ראה, which emphasizes the call to "witness" what Pinchas did to stem the plague of harlotry brought upon the Israelites.

Finally, the three words also tell the story of the Pinchas encounter, as the Israelites "gathered" in front of the "tent" of meeting to weep, as Pinchas created a "boundary" between the Israelite man and Midianite woman to stop the plague.

Notes

Here, there really was only one curiosity, and that related to the different words for "curse" used by Balak, Balaam and God, respectively. Interestingly, each word had multiple synonyms, so there was fertile ground for a midrash. This midrash was the result of playing around with the words and letters until I found something that seemed to work.

PINCHAS

A WISE LEADER SHOULD ALWAYS BE COUNTED AMONG HIS people. So it is written, "And now, O LORD my God, you have made your servant king instead of David my father; and I am but a little child; I know not how to go out or come in. And your servant is in the midst of your people which you have chosen, a great people, that cannot be numbered nor counted for multitude" (I Kings 3:7–8). To what did King Solomon refer when he asked how a king who "know[s] not how to go out or come in" and who "cannot be numbered nor counted for multitude" could be counted "in the midst of [God's] people?" He was asking to be treated like Joshua.

The Torah states, "These are they that were numbered (פקודי) by Moses and Eleazar the priest, who numbered (פקדו) the children of Israel in the plains of Moab by the Jordan at Jericho. But among these [i.e., those numbered in the plains of Moab by the Jordan at Jericho] *there was not a man of them that were numbered* (מפקודי) by Moses and Aaron the priest, who numbered (פקדו) the children of Israel in the wilderness of Sinai. For the LORD had said of them [i.e., those numbered in the wilderness of Sinai]: 'They shall surely die in the wilderness.' *And there was not left a man of them*, save Caleb the son of Jephunneh, and Joshua the son of Nun" (Num. 26:63–65).

The passage therefore states – *on two occasions* – that none who were numbered initially in the wilderness of Sinai were now numbered in the plains of Moab by the Jordan; yet it also says that Joshua nevertheless survived. How are those two statements made consistent? Because Joshua was neither with people "in the wilderness of Sinai" when they were first counted (root פקד), nor with the people "in the plains of Moab by the Jordan at Jericho" when they were counted again (root פקד).

When Moses asks God to appoint a successor, he asks, "Let the LORD, the God of the spirits of all flesh, set a man over the congregation" (Num. 27:16), and he begins his request with the word, "יפקד," which recalls the previous passage. What Moses is truly asking for is that God now "number," or "count," the leader of the congregation. Further, Moses states of his successor (whom God has not yet named), that he "may go out before them, and who may come in before them" (Num. 27:17), reflecting the idea of separation of the leader from the flock. If the leader were in the midst of his people (as Solomon had requested of himself), he would be *already* numbered, and Moses would not have begun his request with the word "יפקד."

God understands the request immediately, and appoints Joshua, who *had not been previously numbered*, saying of him, "at his word shall they go out, and at his word they shall come in, *both he, and all the children of Israel with him*, even all the congregation" (Num. 27:21). And at that, Joshua was put at ease that he would, for the first time, be counted among his people.

$\mathcal{N}otes$

This midrash related the two dominant plot elements of the parasha: the second census of the people, and the appointment of Joshua. The Torah refers to the two different censuses in successive verses, 26:63–64. As to the first, the census in the plains of Moab near Jericho, no one had survived to this point. As to the second, no one had survived, except Caleb and Joshua. This meant Caleb and Joshua had been missing from the first census.

The other language that connected the two involved the phrase, "go out and come in," which appears here in relation to Joshua's appointment, and in Kings (and elsewhere in relation to prophecy). The passage in Kings related to counting as well, and I interpreted it as a request by King Solomon to be counted among his people. That paralleled what was happening in this parasha in relation to Joshua.

MATTOT

THE TORAH SPEAKS OF A SERIES OF ACTS AND CONSE-quences to teach us to treat our souls with moderation.

The Torah speaks of six combinations of a vow of dedication (נדר), an oath (שבעה), a bond of restraint (אסר), and a binding oath (שבעת אסר). Certain combinations of the foregoing lead to certain consequences on the soul, namely, either restraint of the soul (אסרה על-נפשה) or affliction of the soul (ענת נפש). Those combinations, and their source, are:

	Verse (Num.)	Person	Vow of Dedication	And/Or	Oath	Bond of restraint	Binding Oath	Effect on Soul	
								Restrain the soul	Afflict the soul
1	30:3	Man	•	Or	•	•		•	
2	30:4	Unmarried woman in father's house	•	And		•		•	
3	30:7	Married woman in father's house	•	And				•	
4	30:10	Married woman in husband's house	•	And				•	
5	30:11	Widow or Divorced woman	•	Or	•	•		•	

Verse (Num.)	Person	Vow of Dedication	And/Or	Oath	Bond of restraint	Binding Oath	Effect on Soul	
							Restrain the soul	Afflict the soul
6 30:14	All married women	•	And			•		•

What this demonstrates is that:

- **Proposition 1**: a vow of dedication is *always* meant to restrain the soul, because in cases 3 and 4, a vow itself is referred to in connection with restraint of the soul
- **Proposition 2**: an oath to make a bond of restraint is also *always* meant to restrain the soul, because in cases 1 and 5, it can replace a vow to the same effect
- **Proposition 3**: a bond of restraint, by itself, has *no effect* on the soul, since in case 2 the vow itself would have been sufficient and leads to the same result
- **Proposition 4**: a binding oath *always* gives rise to affliction of the soul

Why should God lay out the consequences as such? It is to teach us which activities are proper for the care of the soul, and which are dangerous. First, we should not read "שבעה" as "oath," but rather to refer to its alternative meaning of "satisfaction." Thus:

- When we completely dedicate ourselves to something other than God (Proposition 1), we need to restrain our souls to prevent overzealousness and pride
- When we act for the purpose of pure satisfaction (Proposition 2), we need to restrain our souls from falling into sinfulness
- When we derive satisfaction from restraining ourselves beyond what is demanded of us (Proposition 4), we must afflict our souls with pain so that we can learn to recognize pleasure from the gifts God has given us for the purpose of bringing us joy

- When we act with restraint in worldly matters, neither acting with dedication to things beyond that which God instructs us to dedicate ourselves, nor restraining ourselves to the point of excess pride and satisfaction (Proposition 3), our souls are in the balance God has given us.

Notes

Again, the Torah presents a list of items and combinations associated with actions and consequences. This time, there were so many items and combinations that I literally had to put them in a chart, then sit back and stare at it a while. It became a kind of logic problem at that point. Once the logic was solved, the next step was to find a deeper meaning by understanding what the various categories had to say about people in general.

MASSEY

WHY DOES THE TORAH RECOUNT EACH OF THE encampments wherein the Israelites encamped on their journey in Sinai?

To understand, we must look to the opening of the Book of Numbers, to the beginning of their journey, where the Torah relates, "And the LORD spoke to Moses in the wilderness (במדבר) of Sinai." Do not read במדבר, but instead, בם דבר (or, grammatically proper, בם דבר), "through them He spoke."

What is the meaning of "בם," "through them?" The numerical value of "בם" is 42, which corresponds to the number of encampments recited in the portion. Therefore, God spoke to Moses (and to Israel) through the encampments that they made, for it was through the wilderness experience, and building homes under the new law, that God spoke to Israel and they became a people.

Notes

This may have been the first midrash I ever wrote, predating this Project altogether. I delivered it as a dvar Torah at my synagogue one Shabbat when neither of my synagogue's rabbis were in town. (This parasha often occurs during the summer months around Tisha B'Av when rabbis head

*out for vacation because weddings and bar mitzvahs are traditionally
not performed).*

*I think I counted and re-counted the number of encampments about
a dozen times. I had a horrible feeling after I was finished that someone
would approach me at the Kiddush afterward and say, "Nice thoughts,
but you know, I only counted 41."*

דברים

(Devarim)

DEUTERONOMY

DEVARIM

O N THE BANKS OF THE JORDAN RIVER, MOSES RE-
tells the story of the Israelites' journey. He begins at Horeb
(Sinai), saying "You have dwelled in (שבת ב־) this mountain long enough" (Deut. 1:6). He tells next how the Jewish people
began their journey, only the betrayal of the spies changed their
course of history. As God decreed that the men of that generation
should perish before entering Israel, the Israelites did not heed that
decree and attempted their own conquest, and were vanquished.
Licking their wounds, defeated and decimated, they regrouped at
Mount Seir. There, as Moses recounts, they would begin their Sinai
journey again, with Moses saying, "You have encircled around (סב
את ה־) this mountain long enough" (Deut. 2:3).

Moses' description of the activity at the two mountains is nearly
identical, except that at Sinai he uses the word "שבת," literally to "sit,"
"dwell," or "rest." That is the same word for Shabbat – our holy day
of rest. At Sinai, the Jewish people had experienced the ultimate
"Shabbat," but the resting had gone on long enough. What came
next required "doing," not "resting." At Mount Seir, he uses the word
"סב" instead, literally to "encircle," "encompass," but also "turn." At
Sinai, when they should have been energized, they rested. At Seir,
when they should have been resting after their defeat, they were
turning. Indeed, that generation at Seir had "turned." They had
turned away from God.

Moses recognized this distinction, and his message to the Israelites by using those different phrases was to "turn" again, to keep turning. But to what? Between the phrase "dwell in (שבת ב-)" (totaling 704) and "encircle around (סב את ה-)" (totaling 468) is 236. 236 represents the phrase, מלפני י-ה-ו-ה, "from before the LORD." At Seir, the people had turned, סב, from before the LORD, מלפני י-ה-ו-ה. Going forward, how would they turn back? By recreating their state at Sinai of שבת, Shabbat. Moses' purposeful choice of words told the story of not only the attitude of the Jewish people, but an instruction on how to live when a long journey awaits. Shabbat is the response to our tendency to turn away from before the LORD.

Notes

By the time I had gotten to Devarim, I had taken a long, long break from the Project. I picked it up at one point, focusing on the different language for "dwelled in (שבת ב-)" and "encircled around (סב את ה-)." But I never finished it, and when I came back to this parasha to finish the Project some time later, my notes had reflected that I had played with the words "סב את" to get the words "סבא" ("drunk") and "סבתה" ("grandmother"). It's probably best I had taken a break at that point.

Instead, I focused on the word "סב" and the many references in Scripture to that word meaning "turn" or "turning"(E.g., I Sam. 22:18, II Sam. 18:30, II Kings 9:18). There was a suggestion that "סב" had to do with turning, either a constant turn about an axis, like a circle (thus the translation "encircled about"), but also "turn" as in "turn in another direction." Either translation brought meaning to this passage and helped bring a midrash out of the contrast in terms.

The glue that held it together was the gematria, which helped crystallize what the people were "turning" away from.

VA-ETCHANAN

"BUT CHARGE (וצו) JOSHUA, AND ENCOURAGE (וחזקהו) him, and strengthen (ואמצהו) him; for he shall go over before this people, and he shall cause them to inherit the land which you shall see" (Deut. 3:28).

The three-fold commandment to Moses concerning Joshua defines the evolution of leadership. First Moses is told to "charge (וצויתה)" Joshua (Num. 27:19). In the next passage concerning Joshua, Moses is obliged to "encourage (חזק)" him (Deut. 1:38). In this final passage, Moses is commanded also to "strengthen (ואמצהו)" him.

Joshua's task is to build the Land of Israel from scratch with the Jewish people. The task of building something to sanctify God always comes in three steps: (1) the obligation (צו), (2) the encouragement to prepare and repair (חזק), and finally (3) the strength (אמץ) to see it through.

In that regard, the three-part commandment to Joshua serves as a model for restoring God to His holy places, and making the world fit for His presence. As the Bible relates: "And he [King Joash] gathered together the priests and the Levites, and charged (צאו) them, Go out to the cities of Judah, and collect from all Israel money to repair the house of your God . . . and they hired masons and carpenters to repair (לחזק) the house of the LORD . . . And the workmen labored, and the work prospered in their hand, and they restored the house of God to its proper condition, and strengthened (ויאמצהו) it" (2 Chron. 24:5–13).

Notes

Writing this midrash involved searching the different Scriptural uses of "charge (וצו)," "encourage (וחזקהו)", and "strengthen (ואמצהו)." The passage from Chronicles was the only passage in Scripture that also included all three words.

EKEV

"NOT FOR YOUR RIGHTEOUSNESS, OR FOR THE UP-rightness of your heart, do you go to possess their land; but for the guilt (ברשעת) of these nations the LORD your God drives them out from before you" (Deut. 9:5).

The nations objected to God, "Israel is no more righteous than us, and no more upright of heart. Yet you give them this land on account of *our guilt*. How can we be guilty? It's not our fault you gave Israel your Torah. If you had given it to us, we would have followed it at least as well as they have!"

God responded, "I offered all the nations my Torah, but only Israel responded, 'All that the LORD has spoken we will do' (Ex. 19:8) before they had even heard the laws."

The nations replied, "But they lied to get your Torah! As you said yourself, 'They have quickly turned aside out of the way which I commanded them . . . it is a stiff-necked people; let Me alone that I may destroy them' (Deut. 9:12–14). At least we were honest when we didn't accept your Torah!"

God responded, "But their fathers were superior to your fathers, as it is said, 'Only the LORD took delight in your fathers to love them, and he chose their seed after them, you above all people, *as it is this day*'" (Deut. 10:15).

The nations responded, "But their fathers were many genera-tions ago, and you only visit guilt upon the fourth generation, as you said, 'The LORD, the LORD God, merciful and gracious, long suffering, and abundant in goodness and truth, keeping mercy for thousands, forgiving iniquity and transgression and sin, and that will by no means clear the guilty; visiting the iniquity of the fathers upon the children, and upon the children's children, to the third and to the fourth generation'" (Ex. 34:6–7).

God responded, "But the Israelites have Moses."

The nations responded, "And so what?"

And God said, "When Israel is guilty, they have Moses to intercede on their behalf and remind me that I still love Israel because of their fathers, as Moses said, 'Remember Thy servants, Abraham, Isaac and Jacob: look not unto the stubbornness of this people, nor to their guilt (רשעו), nor to their sin.' (Deut. 9:27). And I responded, 'I have pardoned according to thy word.' (Num. 14:20). Therefore, in every generation I will always pardon Israel according to the word of Moses, as if he had asked me '*as it is this day*.' (Deut. 10:15)"

And the nations wept, because they had none like Moses.

Notes

I particularly liked writing the midrashim with the imagined conversations.

Here, I was surprised by the statement that said God had chosen Israel because they were least of all evils (Deut. 9:5)! This passage cast a whole new light on the concept of a "chosen" people, i.e., "you were chosen because you were less evil than everyone else." Shocking.

Reading that, I could imagine other nations seriously objecting, and I struggled with what God might say to them in response. I knew of the midrash that God had offered the Torah to all the people of the world, but only Israel had accepted it. I now re-imagined that conversation. Fortunately, the parasha also included a little "saving" language, namely, that God's love for Abraham, Isaac and Jacob also was a reason for choosing Israel. That was at least some comfort!

The lynchpin of the imagined midrashic conversation was the passage just after Moses explains that Israel was merely the best of the unrighteous. There, Moses recounts the episode after the spies when God wanted to destroy Israel and make a new people with Moses as their father, and Moses intercedes on Israel's behalf (Deut. 9:12–14). The actual response to that intercession is found in Numbers 14:20. The Torah speaks again and again of Moses' unique ability to convince God to remember his love for Israel. Without that, Israel may have been just like the other nations.

RE'EH

Moses said to Israel, "However (אפס) there shall be no poor among you" (Deut. 15:4).

But God immediately demanded of Moses, "Moses! I did not say אפס! Don't you know that when Scripture says אפס it is associated with lies and deceit?[1] My people will not believe me!"

Moses explained, "But LORD, you have commanded that I tell them, 'Of the non-Jew you shall demand payment, but of your brother's debts you shall release your authority over him' (Deut. 15:3). And then you have commanded that I promise that 'there shall be no poor among you' if you 'perform *this* entire commandment (את כל המצוה) that I command you today' (Deut. 15:5). Because you said את כל המצוה (singular) instead of את כל המצוות (plural), you have made the disappearance of the poor dependent on that one commandment – demanding payment from the non-Jew."

God responded, "So I have."

Moses explained, "But, LORD, the foreign nations are already hostile to your children. So I added אפס so that if they read this

---

1. E.g., Num. 13:28 (the spies' report); Num. 23:13 (Balak's request for a curse from Balaam); Jud. 4:9 (Yael's betrayal of Sisera); II Sam. 12:14 (David's episode with Uriah's wife); Isa. 16:4 (the cursing of extortionists).

passage, they will think that it will not actually come to pass because what you have promised is a lie and deceit."

God responded, "Moses, by your word you have done well. But Israel needs to be reassured. Therefore command my people also, 'For the LORD your God *has blessed you as He has spoken to you*; you will lend to many nations, but you will not borrow; and you will rule many nations, but they will not rule you' (Deut. 15:6). Then they will be reminded that I bless as I speak, and that my word is true."

Notes

There is a noted discrepancy in this parasha. Deuteronomy 15:11 says "the poor shall never cease out of the land." But, Deuteronomy 15:4 says "there shall be no poor among you."

The interesting thing about the statement in 15:4 is the word "אפס," which is roughly translated as, "However," or "Howbeit." In either event, it is an unnecessary word; the remainder of the sentence, if intended to just be taken at face value, makes sense on its own, "there shall be no poor among you."

The interesting thing about "אפס" is its use elsewhere in Scripture. Almost every other use involved some kind of lie or deceit. That couldn't be an accident, and so it allowed the beginning of the midrashic license, and it made more sense when played out in the entire context. Deuteronomy 15:3–5, in its entire context, reads:

> *Of a foreigner you may exact it again [payment of a debt at the jubilee year]; but that which is yours with your brother, your hand shall release. Howbeit there shall be no poor among you; for the Lord shall greatly bless you in the land which the Lord your God gives you for an inheritance to possess it. Only if you carefully listen to the voice of the*

Lord your God, to take care to do this whole commandment which I command you this day.

The singular "commandment (המצוה)" along with the rest of the passage suggested a connection between the poor, the word "אפס" and the collection of debts from non-Jews. With that, I created the midrashic conversation to explain "אפס."

SHOFTIM

"EVEN NOW, BEHOLD, MY WITNESS (עדי) IS IN HEAVEN, and my testimony is on high" (Job 16:19).

If God is the witness, what testimony from man could He need, seeing as He sees all and is just and true? It is because even God cannot condemn to death without a second witness. So we see that God did not destroy the generation of the flood without first consulting Noah, He did not destroy Sodom and Gomorrah without first consulting Abraham, He did not destroy those who made the Golden Calf without first consulting Moses, He did not destroy all of Israel after the spies defied Him without first consulting Moses, He did not destroy Korach and his supporters without first consulting Moses and Aaron, and He did not destroy the sinners in the matter of Baal-Peor without first consulting Moses.

Thus it is written, "but by the mouth of one witness (עד אחד) he shall not be put to death" (Deut. 17:6). The phrase "עד אחד" refers specifically to God, as it is written in the Torah with the letters "ד" and "ע" emphasized,

שמע ישרא־ל יה־ו־ה א־להינו יה־ו־ה אחד

The LORD is One (אחד), and is also Witness (עד). Therefore, we can annul God's decree against us by turning back to Him to avoid being witnesses against ourselves.

137

Notes

Here the interesting text was the phrase "עד אחד" in connection with sentencing a person to death. That phrase had an obvious connection with the Shema. This midrash came out of that.

KI-TETZE

THE TORAH PROVIDES FOR THE FOLLOWING PROCEDURE
when a man accuses his wife of not being a virgin:

(1) The man accuses that there are no signs of her virginity (בתולים)
     (Deut. 22:14)
(2) The wife's parents bring proof to the elders of her virginity (את
     בתולי) (Deut. 22:15)
(3) The parents restate the man's accusation that she has lost her
     virginity (בתולים) (Deut. 22:17)
(4) The parents show the elders the proof of her virginity (בתולי)
     (Deut. 22:17)
(5) If the elders see the proof, they declare her a virgin (בתולת)
     (Deut. 22:19)
(6) If the accusation is true, and they do not find signs of her vir-
     ginity (בתולים), she is stoned (Deut. 22:20)

The woman's virginity is referred to in three different ways: בתולים,
בתולי and בתולת. What is the significance of this?

   When the woman is cast in the most negative light, i.e., by the
accuser, the Torah refers to her virginity using the word "בתולים"
(Deut. 22:14, 17). When the woman is defended, the parents omit

the "מ/ם"[1] and refer to her virginity as "בתולי" (Deut. 22:15, 17). In fact, to the parents, before they state their case to the elders, the Torah tells us that they refer to her virginity as "את בתולי" (Deut. 22:15).

When an accusation against the daughter has been made, it is as if the accuser has stolen the truth (אמת) from them. That is, each parent believes the daughter is "my true virgin (אמת בתולי)," but when the accuser makes the accusation, he steals the מ/ם, and their belief becomes "את בתולי." Thus, the accuser takes the מ/ם and turns the word for virginity to "בתולים."

The elders, if they find her virginity to be true, restore all the truth, referring to her as a virgin, בתולת (Deut. 22:19). In doing so, they take away the "ים" from the accuser's accusation and the "י" from the parents' defense, and they put them together as "ימי," or "all days." Therefore they decree that if the accusation were false, the truth is preserved and the woman shall be the man's wife for "ימיו," i.e., "all his days" (Deut. 22:19).

If, however, the accusation is true, the parents lose that truth forever and her false virginity (בתולים) (Deut. 22:20) is tainted forever by taking away their מ/ם.

Notes

This is another passage with steps and different words to say the same thing at every step. It seems that every time the Torah outlines a detailed legal procedure, there is some linguistic ambiguity thrown into the mix. The striking thing was that the accuser used one term, the parents used another, and the elders yet another. That suggests that the word had to

---

1. See footnote 12.

do with the parties' attitude. Additionally, the language was extremely awkward in that there is not (or at least was not in Biblical times) a word for "virginity." So, all of the references in this parasha to "signs of virginity" seemed to read simply as "virgin." The suffixes added in this parasha, the "ים," "י," and "ת," to the word for "virgin (בתול)," all seemed to convert the word "virgin" to "signs of virginity." Likely, whatever Hebrew grammar rules allowed that are ancient, no longer make sense to the modern reader. (In any event, the Torah never specified what "signs" those would be, but I suppose some things are better left to the imagination).

KI-TAVO

"THESE ARE THE WORDS OF THE COVENANT (דברי הברית) which the LORD commanded to Moses to make with the children of Israel in the land of Moab, besides (מלבד) the covenant which He made with them in Horeb" (Deut. 28:69).

If the curses and blessings given by Moses in Moab were the words of the covenant (דברי הברית), and it was besides (מלבד), i.e., in addition to, the covenant at Sinai (Horeb), then just how many covenants were there between God and the children of Israel?

The Torah refers to five different "words of the covenant (דברי הברית)." They are:

The Covenant with Abraham (Jeremiah 34:18/ Genesis 15:18)	"And I will give the men who have transgressed my covenant, which have not kept the words of the covenant (דברי הברית) which they had made before me, when they cut the calf in two, and passed between its parts" (Jer. 34:18, referring to Gen. 15:17–18 ["And it came to pass, that, when the sun went down, and it was dark, behold a smoking furnace, and a burning torch that passed between those pieces. In the same day the LORD made a covenant with Abram."])

The 10 Commandments	"And he was there with the LORD forty days and forty nights; he did neither eat bread, nor drink water. And he wrote upon the tablets the words of the covenant (דברי הברית), the ten commandments" (Ex. 34:28).
The Sinai Revelation	"Hear the words of this covenant (דברי הברית) . . . cursed be the man who obeys not the words of this covenant (דברי הברית) . . . which I commanded your fathers *in the day that I brought them out of the land of Egypt* (i.e., at Sinai)" (Jer. 11:2).
The Law Code of Deuteronomy	"And the king stood by a pillar, and made a covenant before the LORD, to walk after the LORD, and to keep his commandments and his testimonies and his statutes with all their heart and all their soul, to perform the words of this covenant (דברי הברית) that were written in this book (i.e., the Book of Deuteronomy)" (II Kings 23:3).
The Covenant in Moab	"These are the words of the covenant (דברי הברית) which the LORD commanded to Moses to make with the children of Israel in the land of Moab" (Deut. 28:69).

So what was the nature of each of these covenants?

The Covenant in Moab is beside (מלבד) the other covenants. This relates to the following:

"These are the feasts of the LORD, which you shall proclaim to be holy gatherings, . . . [1] beside (מלבד) the sabbaths of the LORD, and [2] beside (מלבד) your gifts, and [3] beside (מלבד) all your vows, and [4] beside (מלבד) all your freewill offerings, which you give to the LORD" (Lev. 23:37–38). Those four are "besides (מלבד)" the holy festivals, in the same way that the Covenant of Moab is beside (מלבד) the other four covenants.

It can be shown that each of those four aspects of Divine service relates to a covenant above:

your gifts	The Covenant with Abraham ("Abraham gave gifts." Gen. 25:6)
all your vows	The 10 Commandments (the 1st of which is "I am the LORD your God") ("Make a vow and pay to the LORD your God." Ps. 76:12)
the sabbaths of the LORD	The Sinai Revelation ("You have dwelled (שבת) long enough in this mountain." Deut. 1:6)
all your freewill offerings	The Law Code of Deuteronomy (i.e., just before the battle for the Land) ("Your people offer themselves willingly on the day of your battle." Ps. 110:3)

The Covenant at Moab was beside (מלבד) the other covenants, in just the same way the "feasts of the LORD, which you shall proclaim to be holy gatherings (Lev. 23:37–38)," were beside (מלבד) those other manners of observance. Therefore, the Covenant at Moab is equivalent to those "holy gatherings," namely, observance of Rosh Hashanah, Yom Kippur, Sukkot, Passover and Shavuot.

Notes

This was maybe the most difficult parasha I had to write. The entire description of the twelve tribes divided into two camps, one at Mount Ebal to hear curses and one at Mount Gerizim to hear blessings, cried for an interpretation. (Anything involving mountains in the Torah is mysterious). But I couldn't really see anything there.

Instead, I focused on the reference to the "covenant" (Deut. 28:69). Covenants are central to the entire arc of Israel's existence throughout the Torah, and depending on where and when they are, the "covenant" may refer to different things. This passage, through use of the word "besides (מלבד)," made clear that there were, in fact, multiple covenants.

I had two things I needed to search to make sense of this parasha: the word "besides (מלבד)," and the phrase "words of the covenant (דברי הברית)."

As it turns out (as it so often does), there was an intersection: five instances of the use of "words of the covenant (דברי הברית)," and a single passage in the Torah which used the word "besides (מלבד)" repetitively. Having those two things together meant only finding a way to match them up.

NITZAVIM

"THE HIDDEN THINGS (הנסתרת) BELONG UNTO THE LORD our God; the things that are revealed (והנגלת) belong to us and our children forever" (Deut. 29:28).

This refers to the Messiah, the anointed one of David, whose existence belongs to us, but whose time is known only to God. How do we know that this passage refers to the Messiah? Because in the entirety of Scripture, only David is spoken of as being hidden (I Sam. 20:5) ("And David said to Jonathan . . . 'let me go, that I may hide myself (ונסתרתי) in the field . . .'"), as well as revealed (II Sam. 6:20) ("And Michal the daughter of Saul came out to meet David, and said, 'How glorious was the king of Israel today, who revealed himself (נגלה) today . . .'").

Notes

This one was relatively simple. When I searched for "hidden (הנסתרת)" and "revealed (והנגלת)," David was the only person (or thing) that showed up for each.

VAYELECH

THE TORAH USES THE PHRASE "וילך משה (AND MOSES went)" exactly four times: twice at the very beginning of Moses' call to prophecy, and twice at the very end. In each case, the Torah states "וילך משה (And Moses went)" first with respect to Moses alone, and the second time with a partner – Aaron in the beginning, and Joshua at the end.

The passages are as follows:

The Beginning of His Prophecy

Exodus 4:18:   וילך משה ("And Moses went and returned to Jethro his father-in-law, and said to him, 'Let me go, I beseech you, and return to my brothers who are in Egypt'").

Exodus 4:29–30:   וילך משה ("And Moses and Aaron went and gathered together all the elders of the people of Israel; And Aaron spoke all the words which the LORD had spoken to Moses, and did the signs in the sight of the people.")

The End of His Prophecy

Deut. 31:1–2:   וילך משה ("And Moses went and spoke these words to all Israel. And he said to them, 'I am one hundred and twenty years old this day; I can no more go out and come in'").

Deut. 31:14:   וילך משה ("And Moses and Joshua went, and presented themselves in the Tent of Meeting.")

At the beginning of his prophecy, "Moses went" alone, in order to "go . . . and return" to do his work. Then "Moses went" with Aaron to do his work "in the sight of the people" (Ex. 4:29–30). This demonstrates that one who accepts leadership should do so with pride and publicity.

At the end of his prophecy, "Moses went" alone, but, unlike the beginning of his prophecy when he went to "go . . . and return," now he could no longer "go out and come in." The phrase "I can no more go out and come in" is written, לא אוכל עוד לצאת ולבוא, the first letters of which spell "לא עלו," or "no yoke." This refers to God's relieving Moses of having to carry Israel's burden of transgressions any longer, so that he could die in peace, as it says, "The yoke (עלו) of my transgressions is bound by his hand; they are knit together and are set upon my neck; he has caused my strength to fall, the LORD has delivered me into the hands of those against whom I am not able to rise up" (Lam. 1:14). At that point, "Moses went" with Joshua, but this time God allowed him to retire in privacy to protect his honor, i.e., they "presented themselves in the Tent of Meeting."

Notes

The phrase "Moses went" seemed to be superfluous. The Torah doesn't tell us where he went, or why. At the same time, it uses the familiar phrase about prophecy, "going out and coming in."

Interestingly, the Torah uses "Moses went (וילך משה)" just at the beginning and end of his prophecy, and the parallels to both were striking.

The last part of the midrash was to make sense of the phrase, used frequently in respect of prophecy, "I can no more go out and come in" (לא אוכל עוד לצאת ולבוא). The acronym for that phrase, "לא עלו," worked.

HAAZINU

C AN A MAN SEE GOD'S FACE?
The Torah gives different answers.
In some instances, God plainly shows His face, as in, "The LORD will make His face shine upon you" (Num. 25:6). Or, "For the LORD is righteous, He loves righteousness, the upright (ישר) shall behold His face" (Ps. 11:7). Or, "And I will not hide My face from them anymore, for I have poured out My spirit upon the house of Israel" (Ezek. 39:29).

But other instances suggest the opposite. For example, when Moses pleads and argues with God to know His essence, an angry God responds, "Man shall not see My face and live" (Ex. 33:23). And, in the course of Moses' final poem describing an ungrateful and sinful Israel, Israel is told, "I will hide My face from them" (Deut. 32:20).

This last example is most puzzling, as God is speaking about Jeshurun (ישרון), another name for Israel connoting their nobility and "uprightness (ישר)." Yet, in the passage above from Psalms, we see that God will make His face seen by ישר, i.e., "the upright (ישר) shall behold His face." So, how could God "hide My face from Jeshurun (ישרון)," while "the upright (ישר) shall behold His face?"

Another passage reconciles these statements. "'In overflowing wrath I hid My face from you for a moment; but with everlasting

kindness will I have mercy on you,' says the LORD your redeemer"
(Isa. 54:8).

Thus, God hides His face *only* "in overflowing wrath," and *only*
"for a moment." It is because of His overflowing wrath in the moment that "man shall not see My face and live," as who could withstand God's wrath? To whom does God show His face? To those who
do not incur his wrath, that is, the upright (ישר), Jeshurun (ישרון),
upon whom He has poured out His spirit.

Notes

The Biblical term for Israel, Jeshurun, appears for the first time in this
parasha. Normally, Jeshurun is a name of honor, but here Jeshurun is used
in the context of God hiding His face. In addition, the name Jeshurun
(ישרון) is based on the root, "ישר," meaning "upright," a word that appears
throughout the parasha. This set up the conflict to be solved by midrash:
God would hide His face from Jeshurun, but not withhold His face from
the upright (Ps. 11:7).

The idea of God revealing Himself and hiding His face appears
throughout Scripture, and whether He does one or the other depends on
which book, and the context. Despite the statement in Exodus to Moses
that no man "shall see my face and live" (Ex. 33:20–23), that was clearly
not an absolute statement. How one would see God's face needed to be
reconciled in the context of this midrash. The passage from Isaiah was
directly on point.

VEZOT HA-BERACHAH

AT THE END OF THE TORAH, MOSES COMPLETES HIS blessings, and in the final passage (Deut. 34:1–12), we are told that Moses dies and is buried on Mount Nebo, and no man knows where. We are told Israel mourned for thirty days, and Joshua assumed the mantle of leadership.

If Moses died, and his whereabouts were unknown, who wrote the last passage of the Torah about his death and what happened after? If Moses wrote it, as he was dying, it would have been lost, as no one would have been able to find it because Moses' whereabouts were forever unknown.

The possibilities are:

(1) Moses wrote it in advance and left it with the Levites as part of the Book he deposited beside the Ark of the Covenant (Deut. 31:9) ("And Moses wrote this Torah, and delivered it to the priests the sons of Levi, who carried the ark of the covenant of the LORD, and to all the elders of Israel.")

or

(2) Joshua wrote it on his own because his prophecy began as soon as Moses went up to Mount Nebo to die.

The Torah relates, concerning Joshua, that he was "full of the spirit of wisdom, for Moses had laid his hands upon him" (Deut. 34:9).

However, when Joshua is first appointed, the Torah states, "And the LORD said to Moses, Take Joshua the son of Nun, a man in whom is spirit, and lay your hand upon him" (Num. 27:18).

When Joshua is first appointed, he had only spirit. When his prophecy officially begins, he has spirit and wisdom. What had he gained when he gained wisdom? He gained the entire Torah, as it is written, "This (i.e., the Torah) is your wisdom" (Deut. 4:6). Therefore, Joshua had gained the prophecy necessary to complete the Torah after Moses' death.

Notes

Rabbinic literature addressed the authorship of Deuteronomy and its various parts at different points.[1] I wasn't breaking new ground here with the idea that Joshua wrote the last twelve verses of Deuteronomy. But, in all of that literature, I had not seen an explanation for how Joshua commenced his prophetic mission.

When Joshua was appointed successor, the Torah refers to his "spirit" (Num. 27:18). Here, the Torah refers to "the spirit of wisdom" that is in him (Deut. 34:9). The addition of the word "wisdom" is significant, as "wisdom" is associated throughout Scripture, rabbinic and Kabbalistic literature with Torah. The addition of the word "wisdom" here provided the explanation for how Joshua was able to actually write the Torah.

1. See Heschel, R. Abraham J., *Torah Min Hashamayim: Heavenly Torah: As Refracted Through the Ages*, Levin and Tucker, eds. and trans., Continuum Int'l Pub. Group Inc. (2007), pp. 451-77, 610-38.

INDEX OF BIBLICAL CITATIONS

The citation is followed by the page number on which it appears.

GENESIS

7:7 22
12:1 106
12:7 24
12:8 24
12:9 24
12:10 24
13:3–4 25
13:18 29
15:5 26
15:17–18 142
15:18 142
18:21 26
22:2 27, 75
22:17–18 27
22:19 28

23:2 28
23:12 28–29
23:40 29
25:6 144
25:21 31
26:5 31
26:12 26
26:18 30
26:19–21 30
26:22 30
26:32 30
27:1 44
28:11 32
28:13–15 32
28:16 32
49:1 44

28:17 32
28:18 32
32:23 36
32:24 35
32:24–25 34
32:25 35
32:30 34
32:31 34
35:1 35
35:6 34
35:11 35
35:15 35
37:2 39
37:4 37, 38
37:5 37, 38
50:15 45

37:8 37, 38
37:11 38
42:1 39
42:2 39
44:17 39
45:1 39
45:7 42
45:27 40
45:28 41
46:3–4 41
46:30 41
47:9 41
48:1–2 45
48:10 44
48:11 44

EXODUS

2:14 70
2:23 49, 50
3:1 49
4:18 147
4:26 86
4:29–30 147,

148
6:5 51
6:7 51
6:8 51
6:9 51
6:12 70

10:16–17 55
10:17 54
10:21 54, 55
10:22 54
13:14 93
13:16 93

14:4 57
14:11 57
14:12 57
14:19–20 56
15:4 58
15:5 58

15:19 22
17:3 70
19:6 67
19:8 62, 131
19:9 59
19:11 59
19:18 59
19:19 59
21:8 108
22:19 63

24:16 71
24:3 62, 63
24:7 62
24:9 67, 68
25:2 64
25:22 64
25:30 64
28:1 67, 68
28:35 83, 84
31:17 65
40:33 74, 76

32:1 69
32:19 70
33:20–23 150
33:23 149
34:6–7 132
34:14 103
34:28 143
34:30 69
35:30 72
35:31 72
40:35 76

38:21 75
40:8 76
40:9 74, 76
40:19 74
40:21 74
40:23 74
40:25 74
40:27 74
40:29 74
40:32 74

LEVITICUS

4:2 79, 80
4:13 79
4:22 79
4:27 79
6:10 81
6:18 81
7:1 81
7:6 81
10 24
10:1 83
12:2–4 85

12:5 85
14:12 88
14:57 87
16:2 89
16:13 89
19:2 91, 92, 103
19:4 92
19:10 92
19:12 92
19:14 92
19:16 92

19:18 92
19:21 92
19:25 91
19:30 92
19:31 91
19:32 92
19:34 91
19:36 91
19:37 92
20:4 92
20:8 92
26:41–42 97

23:14 93
23:21 93
23:31 93
23:37–38 143, 144
23:41 94
24:6 64
24:8 64
25:10 95, 96
25:13 95
25:23 95, 96

NUMBERS

1:2 101
1:3 101, 102
3:4 67, 68
5:13 103
5:31 103
7:89 104
9:17 105, 106
9:18 105, 106
9:19 105, 106
9:20 105, 106
9:21 105, 106
9:22 105, 106
30:10 120

9:23 105, 106
13:2 108
13:19 108
13:28 134
14:4 112
14:20 132, 133
14:37 109
16:32 114
16:6 70
17:2 110, 111
17:3 110
17:4 110
30:11 123

17:6 110
17:17 110–111
20:22 113, 114
20:24 113
20:25 113
20:26 113
20:27 113
20:28 113
22:5 90
22:6 115
22:11 115
22:12 115
30:14 121

23:13 134
25:6 149
25:8 115
26:63–65 117, 118
27:16 120
27:17 120
27:18 152
27:19 131
27:21 118
30:3 120
30:4 120
30:7 120

DEUTERONOMY

1:6 127, 144
1:38 129
2:3 127
3:28 129
4:6 152
4:29 24
6:8 65
9:5 131, 132

9:12–14 131, 133
9:27 132
10:15 131, 133
15:3 134
15:3–5 135–136
15:4 134, 135
15:5 134
15:6 135

15:11 135
17:6 137
22:14 139
22:15 139, 140
22:17 139, 140
22:19 139, 140
22:20 139
28:69 142, 143,

144, 145
29:28 146
31:1–2 147
31:9 151
31:14 147
32:20 149
34:1–12 151
34:7 32

34:9 151, 152

JUDGES
4:9 134

I SAMUEL
2:7 83, 84   20:5 146   22:18 128

II SAMUEL
6:20 146   12:14 134   18:30 128

I KINGS
19:12 59
3:7–8 117

II KINGS
9:18 128   28:3 143

ISAIAH
6:1 71
10:20–22 42
16:4 134

16:5 90
24:21 102
29:10 90

35:10 49
51:1–2 25
54:8 149–150

56:12 93
60:19–22 56
61:1–2 75

JEREMIAH

7:22–23 65	18:20 30	31:32–34 60	33:22 101, 102
11:2 143	18:22 30	33:11 83	34:18 142
		49:12 103	

EZEKIEL

10:5 62   39:29 40, 149   44:28 95, 96

HABAKKUK

3:3 89

ZECHARIAH

14:9 103

PSALMS

6:16 69–70	23:3 34	65:3–4 94	110:3 144
11:7 149, 150	57:7 30	65:12 94	119:85 30
19:4–9 62	65:12 95	76:12 144	133:1–2 44
	137:18 26, 27	139:17 26	

PROVERBS

6:16 69	6:34 38	12:16 90	27:4 37

JOB

16:19 137	23:15–17 90	26:9 89	37:16 28

LAMENTATIONS

5:21 87

2 CHRONICLES

24:5–13 129–130

About the Author

Daniel Shulman was named one of the top 40 lawyers under 40 in Illinois by the Law Bulletin and is the author of *Insights Hurt: Bringing Healing Thoughts to Life*. He lives in a suburb of Chicago, Illinois with his three sons, Elijah, Noah and Micah.